*Bride's · Little · Book · of*

# VOWS
*and*
# RINGS

CLARKSON POTTER / PUBLISHERS NEW YORK

# *acknowledgments*

BRIDE'S especially wants to thank KATHY MULLINS, the books's writer and researcher, for exploring the many ways a couple may pledge their troth. Many thanks, too, to ANDREA FELD, BRIDE'S Managing Editor, for her invaluable contribution to the outline and content of the book. Heartfelt appreciation to ROCHELLE UDELL and MARY MAGUIRE of The Condé Nast Publications Inc., for making this book happen, to LAUREN SHAKELY of Clarkson N. Potter, and to BRIDE'S Art Director PHYLLIS RICHMOND COX. Applause to DENISE O'DONOGHUE, BRIDE'S Beauty Editor; RACHEL LEONARD, BRIDE'S Fashion Editor; and DONNA FERRARI, BRIDE'S Tabletop, Food and Wine Editor, for originally styling many of the photographs in this book for publication in the magazine. Appreciation to staff member Mary Catherine McCooey, for arranging photographers' and other permissions, and to Denise Evans, for her computer wizardry.

*Photographers :* Jaime Biondo (pgs. 26-27); Pascal Chevallier (pg. 29); Michael Grand (pg. 39); Douglas Keeve (pgs. 11, 19); Yoshi Onaya (pgs. 20, 22-23, 24-25); Patrice Reumont (pg. 33); Alan Richardson (cover, pgs. 4, 7, 8, 13, 30, 34); Bico Stupakoff (pg. 16); William Waldron (pg. 43).

*Vows :* Portions of Scripture from Revised Standard Version, © Division of Christian Education, National Council of Churches, 1971. Verse from "Song of Songs," and traditional Jewish ring vow cited in The Jewish Wedding Book, by Rabbi Daniel B. Syme (Pharos Books, 1991). Excerpts from the Rite of Marriage, © 1969 by the International Committee on English in the Liturgy, Inc. Carpatho-Russian Orthodox and Muslim vows cited in Weddings: A Guide to All Religious & Interfaith Marriage Services, by Abraham J. Klausner (Alpha Publishing Co., 1986). Portions of religious vows cited in Into the Garden: A Wedding Anthology, Robert Hass and Stephen Mitchell (HarperCollins Publishers, 1993). Every effort has been made to locate the copyright owners of material used in this book. Please contact BRIDE'S magazine if any oversight or error has been made.

*Rings :* Steven Krechmer (pg. 20); Louis Glick Diamond Corporation (pgs. 22-23, 24-25); David S. Kwiat, Stuart More, Ltd., Suberi Brothers, The Diamond Information Center (pgs. 24-25); The World Gold Council (pgs. 26-27); Tiffany & Co. (pg. 29).

*Additional Credits :* Doily favor design, Anne-Stuart Hamilton (pg. 34). Dresses, Christine & Co. (pg. 16); Jean Pheonix (pg. 33); Jessica McClintock (pg. 11). Flowers, Christopher Bassett, N.Y.C. (pgs. 7, 8); Valerie Hart Designs, N.Y.C. (pg. 13). Marriage medallion, Westport Allen Center, Clergy Services, Kansas City, MO. (pg. 39). Ring pillow, Fortunoff (cover).

Published by Clarkson N. Potter, Inc., 201 East 50th Street, New York, New York 10022. Member of the Crown Publishing Group. CLARKSON N. POTTER, POTTER and colophon are trademarks of Clarkson N. Potter, Inc. Random House, Inc. New York, Toronto, London, Sydney, Auckland
Manufactured in Hong Kong.

Design by Justine Strasberg

Library of Congress Cataloging-in-Publication Data
Bride's little book of vows and rings/by the editors of Bride's magazine.
   p. cm.
1. Marriage service.   2. Jewelry.   3. Gems.   I. Bride's (The Condé Nast Publications Inc.)
II. Title: Little book of vows and rings.
HQ745.B786  1994
392'.5—dc20                                93-25802
                                          CIP

ISBN 0-517-59678-4
10  9  8  7  6  5  4

_contents_

Set me as a seal upon your heart"—a passionate plea from the lyrical <u>Song of Songs</u>. With that signet marker—a seal—a contract or a love letter is finalized. Weddings put that stamp of authenticity on relationships—with timeless and timely vows; with solemn rituals such as processions; and, symbolic sharing of wine and rings and families.

In every culture, important occasions have traditions, rituals, and even laws associated with them. There is little need to speak the language to understand a country's wedding traditions, for symbolism crosses cultural lines. The <u>exchange of rings</u>, the participation of family and friends, the presence of an authority figure, all play a role in sanctifying the union.

*introduction*

Family networks bond through celebration of <u>ethnic traditions</u> and expression of shared values. Readings are chosen with care and speakers are honored participants. A father reading an inspirational passage is defining his family; a brother's song signals the caring bond that will continue.

Not content to let ancient liturgies frame their marriages, couples labor over wedding <u>words</u>. These are not the words of wooing, or long-range planning; these are expressions of commitment, awesome in their significance. While echoing generations of human history, words define this unique pair.

We applaud the efforts of wedding couples to redefine their loving relationships through ceremony. Couples today understand as few generations before, that the "seal" on their <u>wedding</u> is not a period, but a comma. The story of their <u>marriage</u> goes on and on...each chapter composed of words scripted day by day in little acts of kindness and generosity.

BARBARA TOBER

Editor–in–Chief, BRIDE'S magazine

The bride and groom marry each other in the presence of witnesses by making a public sign of commitment — spoken or symbolic. Civil or religious officiants sanctify, bless, record, but do not "marry" the couple.

In the first century, Christian and Jewish couples wed by reciting a simple public vow, such as, "Be thou consecrated to me," and exchanging a ring. But the Church began to impose requirements on these rites and by the 11th century, marriage became a Catholic sacrament. A rabbinical or priestly blessing was not required until the 15th century.

*what is a vow?*

Throughout history, vows remained remarkably similar. A 14th-century Missal instructs the bridegroom to say: "Ich JOHN, take the JANE, to my wedded wife, to haven and to holden, for fayrere, for fouler, for bettur for wors, for richer for porer..."

Eloquent without speaking vows, the Japanese wed at a Shinto shrine by sipping three times from each of three cups of sake. African slaves said "we're married" by Jumping the Broom, a public commitment for those forbidden to marry. Sharing (eating together) or binding (tying wrists or fingers) are other ways to say "I do."

# *the wedding service*

Most ceremonies include: Prelude, Procession, Call to Worship, Charge to Couple, Presentation, Vows, Exchange of Rings, Nuptial Blessing, Kiss, Recession.

The <u>Call to Worship</u> is the welcome that sets the tone and states the significance of the ceremony:

❧ *"Dearly Beloved: We have come together in the presence of God to witness and bless the joining together of this man and this woman in Holy Matrimony."* — EPISCOPAL

❧ *"May the One who is mighty and blessed above all bless the groom and the bride."* —JEWISH

❧ *"My dear friends, you have come together in this church so that the Lord may seal and strengthen your love in the presence of the Church's minister and this community...."* —ROMAN CATHOLIC

The <u>Charge to the Couple</u> determines that the parties are marrying of their own free wil:

❧ *"Will you have this man to be your wedded husband to live together in holy matrimony? Will you love him, comfort him, honor and keep him in sickness and in health, in sorrow and in joy, and forsaking all others, be faithful to him as long as you both shall live?"* —PROTESTANT

❧ *"Have you come here freely and without reservation to give yourselves to each other in marriage? Will you love and honor each other as man and wife for the rest of your lives?..."* —ROMAN CATHOLIC

At the <u>Presentation</u>, individuals leave their past affiliation to form a new family unit and parents pledge support:

❧ *"Will you, parents of this man and woman, give your blessings to their union?"* —PROTESTANT

❧ *"Who gives the (bride / groom) in marriage?" "(She) gives (herself), and we share (her) giving, joyfully."* —UNITARIAN

*religious vows*

❧ *"I, Jane, take you, John, to be my husband. I promise to be true to you in good times and bad, in sickness and in health. I will love you and honor you all the days of my life."*
— ROMAN CATHOLIC

❧ *"I, John, take you, Jane, as my wedded wife, and I promise you love, honor, and respect; to be faithful to you, and not to forsake you until death do us part. So help me God, one in the Holy Trinity, and all the Saints."* — CARPATHO-RUSSIAN ORTHODOX

❧ *"I am the word and you are the melody. I am the melody and you are the word."* — TRADITIONAL HINDU MANTRA

❧ "I, Jane, choose you, John, to be my husband — my friend, my love, the father of our children. I will be yours in plenty and in want, in sickness and in health, in failure and in triumph. I will cherish you and respect you, comfort and encourage you and together we shall live, freed and bound by our love."

— PROTESTANT

❧ "We will all, verily, abide by the will of God."

— BAHA'I FAITH

❧ "Jane, I take you to be my wife; to laugh with you in joy; to grieve with you in sorrow; to grow with you in love; serving mankind in peace and hope; as long as we both shall live."

— UNITED CHURCH OF CANADA

❧ "I pledge, in honesty and with sincerity, to be for you an obedient and faithful wife." (Bride)

"I pledge, in honesty and sincerity, to be for you a faithful and helpful husband." (Groom)

— MUSLIM

# vows for exchange of rings

❧ "With this ring I thee wed, with my body I thee worship, and with all my worldly goods, I thee endow."
— PROTESTANT

❧ "Behold you are consecrated unto me with this ring, according to the law of Moses and Israel." — JEWISH

❧ "This ring I give you, in token and pledge of our constant faith and abiding love." — PRESBYTERIAN

❧ "I give this ring to you, my beloved, my friend, my wife / husband." — UNITED CHURCH OF CHRIST

❧ "I give you this ring as a symbol of my vow, and with all that I am, and all that I have, I honor you, in the name of the Father, and of the Son, and of the Holy Spirit." — PROTESTANT EPISCOPAL

❧ "I give you this ring as a sign of my love and faithfulness." — AMERICAN LUTHERAN

❖ RING FINGER  Egyptians wore wedding rings on the middle finger of the left hand; ancient Romans believed that the vein in the third finger of the left hand ran directly to the heart. Medieval bridegrooms invoked the Holy Trinity while placing the ring first on the thumb; then index and middle fingers, and finally on the third finger, left hand, sounding "Amen." Puritans disapproved of a ring in the ceremony; it quietly appeared on the bride's hand afterward. In some European countries, wedding rings are worn on the right hand. A Greek woman wears her ring on her left hand while engaged; on the right, after marriage. A Jewish bride receives hers on the right index finger, so it will be visible to witnesses.

❖ DOUBLE-RING CEREMONIES  Coin breaking, to mark a betrothal, implied that a couple must stick to their commitment because each holding half, they are worth more together than apart. Similar in spirit. the double-ring exchange has roots in Northern Europe and was copied in this country by returning servicemen after World War II. In the Jewish faith, double-ring ceremonies are found in Reform and some Conservative services.

*ring folklore*

The engaging custom of the diamond ring dates back to 1477 when Emperor Maximilian of Austria proposed to Mary of Burgundy with a gold ring festooned with diamonds. Rare and extremely precious, diamonds were an indulgence of the aristocracy until 1870, when large deposits were discovered in Africa and the diamond, once reserved for kings and emperors, became the gemstone of choice for millions of brides.

❖ RING LORE  It's unlucky to take one's wedding ring off. ❖ It's unlucky to drop the ring on the floor during the wedding ceremony. ❖ A Jewish man gives his bride a plain gold band so she will not be misled by his wealth. ❖ No one but the bride should try on a wedding ring, or her future will be unhappy. ❖ If the wedding ring breaks, or the stone is lost, there will be a quarrel or separation. ❖ According to legend, Prometheus was the first ring maker, smelting metal in the fire he stole from the gods.

❖ THE MEANING OF DIAMONDS  Diamonds, produced by thunderbolts, protected the wearer from disease and evil, and granted the wearer courage. Greeks believed the stones to be tears of the gods; the gems' inner fire, a reflection of love's passion  Romans thought Cupid's arrows were tipped with diamonds, splinters from stars. To claim the magic, a diamond must be found "naturally," not bought, unless given as a pledge of love.

❖ THE MEANING OF GEMSTONES  ❖ Sapphires, representing purity, are the color of heaven and protect the wearer against dark spirits, such as envy. The blue sapphire changes color when worn by an unfaithful mate. ❖ Emeralds are symbols of faithfulness, immortality, and youth. ❖ Rubies are gems of the sun; thus, the fire inside always shines to guard the home and provide a life of peace and health. ❖ Topaz has the qualities of long life, beauty, intelligence. ❖ Amethysts are lucky gemstones and keep bad magic at bay. ❖ Lapis lazuli guard against fever and vertigo. ❖ Opals turn pale when near poison and dispel melancholy; but, because they change colors so easily, opals represent inconstancy. ❖ Turquoise brings wealth when one gazes at it after a new moon. ❖ Jade, the Chinese believe, is a stone of good fortune and physical well-being.

*Marquise*

*Oval*

❖ MARQUISE gems are oblong with pointed ends. The cut is named for Madame de Pompadour, renowned marquise, duchess and mistress of Louis XV. ❖ OVAL is an adaptation

*stone shapes*

of the round-cut diamond and appears larger than a round stone of the same carat weight. ❖ ROUND, or brilliant, is the most popular and traditional cut. Its 58 facets (tiny planes) enable it to reflect more light than the other common cuts. ❖ PEAR-SHAPED diamonds are round on one end, pointed on the other (the point is worn toward the

*Round*

*Emerald*

*Pear*

fingernail). The name comes from the French word <u>pende-loque</u> related to the English <u>pendant</u>. ❖ EMERALD-CUT diamonds—considered the most formal—are rectangular, with "steps" on the sides and corners. Other cuts (not pictured):
❖ HEART-SHAPED diamonds are a romantic variance on the pear-shaped stone. ❖ BAGUETTE, small and rectangular-shaped, with square corners, is often used beside a larger stone to enhance the overall appearance. ❖ PAVÉ diamonds are small stones fitted into tapered holes, placed very close together to form a continuous surface. ❖ FANCY CUT describes the shape of any cut except round.

Know the qualities that set diamonds apart from one another. The 4 C's are used to determine price, value, and desirability. ❖ CUT refers to a diamond's overall proportions. Shape, cutting style, proportions, and finish are

## *the 4c's of diamonds*

considered. A well-cut stone will appear more brilliant; one that is poorly cut tends to look lifeless. ❖ CLARITY refers to a gem's freedom from natural flaws, such as inner cracks, bubbles, specks, which are hard to detect with the naked eye. Grades range from FL (flawless) to I3 (imperfect). Few diamonds are truly flawless. The higher the clarity of the diamond, the more it will cost. ❖ COLOR is defined on a letter scale, ranging from D (absolutely colorless) to Z (yellow), using standards set by

the Gemological Institute of America. Most diamonds contain slight traces of yellow or brown. Clear white diamonds are the most expensive. ❖ CARAT weight is the standard measure of a diamond's size. One carat weighs 100 points. This system of measuring diamond weight began in India and was based on the predictably uniform seeds of the carob tree. ❖ CERTIFICATION is a process developed for giving written proof of a diamond's weight, grade, and identifying characteristics, by the International Gemological Institute.

✣ *Rings: (1,2) Stackable heart-shaped, diamond-studded rings; (3) Matte finish with baguettes; (4) Tension band displays full diamond; (5) Small uniform stones in channel setting; (6) Heart-shaped diamond band; (7) Wide pavé-diamond band; (8) Man's textured-diamond band; (9) Sculpted band, pear-shaped diamond; (10) Florentine band, round diamond studs; (11) Starburst diamond with trillion-cut diamonds; (12) Heart-shaped diamond with baguettes.*

*Appliquéd*

*Hammered*

*Handbraided*

*Engraved*

*Matte*

*Diamond-cut*

*Milgrained*

## *bands of gold*

❖ BANDS are designed in platinum, yellow or white gold, with simple polished, or subtle matte finishes. Some sport hammered or appliquéd designs or diamond-cut (etched) finishes. Whether flat or curved, unadorned, or gem-studded, bands should be comfortable to wear. ❖ CONTEMPORARY ALTERNATIVES to traditional wedding bands express individuality, with carvings of flowers; diamond groupings; geometric designs; gemstones. Gold settings are braided, twisted, or tied up in a bow. Other options: settings in which stones are set flush in the metal; "rattle" rings, in which small diamonds fill a hidden compartment in the gold band. ❖ SETS AND SETTINGS are chosen with an eye to the shape of the bride's hand. Tiny hands look best with a narrow band, a single-stone engagement ring. Square hands require a slim design, such as a pear or marquise stone. Larger hands, longer fingers, can wear more elaborate rings. If the engagement ring is an unusual shape, the wedding band should conform to it. Some choose a larger band that is worn separately.

❖ HIS RING There's nothing new about men wearing engagement rings. In Elizabethan times, men shared a <u>gimmel ring</u> with the bride-to-be. The parts were reunited as her wedding ring. Men's wedding rings became popular during World War II, when soldiers wanted to carry a token of home. Today, some men prefer bands with subtle detailing, while others choose diamond rings; grooms opt for smaller diamonds set into the band, or a splash of diamonds on top of the ring.

*High-polish*

*Embossed*

*Florentine*

*Repoussé*

*Satin*

*Granulated*

Set a budget. Diamond rings are available in all price ranges. The figure often used is two months of the groom's salary. ❖ Select a jeweler whose reputation you trust. Check with the Better Business Bureau and find out how long they have been in business. ❖ Ask questions. Is there a return or replacement policy? Will the jeweler guarantee his claims in writing? Is there a gemologist on staff?

*shopping tips*

Will they provide an appraisal? ❖ Check credentials. Ask if the jeweler is a member of the American Society of Appraisers, the American Gem Society. ❖ Don't make your purchase in stores that make you uncomfortable. Avoid stores with pushy salespeople, counters with colored lights (they're designed to make inferior diamonds look more impressive). ❖ Learn the lingo. Gold is described in karats, units of weight which express the proportion of gold to alloy (24 karat is 100% gold). Wedding bands range from 14- to 18-karat gold. Silver, copper, nickel, and zinc are common alloys combined to strengthen the beautiful but soft metal. ❖ Get an independent appraisal to verify the jeweler's claim of value. Choose an MGA (Master Gemologist Appraiser) or CGA (Certified Gemologist Appraiser).

Start soon. There will be many other concerns close to the wedding day. ❖ Understand the meaning of traditional vows before departing from them. You may choose to vary, rather than replace. ❖ Speak to your officiant about what's acceptable; ask for resources. ❖ Attend weddings and jot down observations. Collect phrases. ❖ Think about the obligations, rewards of marriage; your partner's best traits; your uncertainties; your understanding of marriage. Put

*writing your vows*

thoughts into promises. ❖ Don't be tempted to say everything. Part of the beauty of the traditional vows is the eloquent brevity. ❖ Preserve the reverence. Weddings are not just personal, they occur in a continuum of community and family expectations. ❖ Speak to each other. Be sure what you are planning to say will not embarrass your partner. ❖ Read aloud, listening to the cadence. The rhythm should be pleasing; the phrasing, easy to understand. ❖ Print words in a wedding program, so everyone can reflect on them later.

**INTERCULTURAL** *"Our love has opened windows to the worlds we lived in as children. I have profound respect for your heritage; but, I am not part of it. We have vowed to live our adult lives together. Our marriage will be a new creation. Now I promise to build bridges of understanding and share the best of myself with your family, your friends, and you."*

# contemporary vows

**INTERFAITH** *"I have enjoyed the time we've spent talking about what our different faiths mean to us. We have discovered much that we share in common. It is my prayer that the candles we've lit together today in unity will enlighten our path to the future. I promise to honor your traditions as I honor you."*

**REMARRIAGE** *"I marry you with my eyes wide open. You have helped me let go of the past and embrace the future. Thank you for making me laugh again. Bless you for taking my hand as I begin anew."*

**HOLIDAY WEDDING** *"There is no better reason to give thanks this Thanksgiving (Christmas) than for discovering God's grace in another human being. Loving you has enriched my soul. With reverence and humility I become your wife. I will cherish you, learn and grow with you, and never cease to give thanks that we found each other."*

**GOLDEN YEARS** *"I offer you not the 'summer of my life,' but the autumn, brisk and vibrant. I promise to be a companion worthy of your precious friendship. I pledge you compassion in good times and bad; encouragement in sickness and health. It is my intent that our life together include our large circle of friends and our loving families. We'll cherish the memories of our individual pasts; and create our new life as we go along — together."*

*sample vows*

**REAFFIRMATION** *"Twenty years ago, when the future stretched out before us like an untraveled highway, I vowed to love you through thick and thin. We set off on a wonderful adventure which had its share of detours and roadside catastrophes. We're still travelers. And today it's just as thrilling to spend a day with you as it was when we first married ... that's why 'I still do.'"*

✦ *(Left:) Lacy doilies wrap candied almond favors for guests.*

**❧ TWO CAREERS** *"The paths we've each taken to get here have now converged. The best promise I can make today is to continue to become the best man that I can be. You too are a unique person and I will encourage you in every way to use your talents. I vow to do all that I can to make our home a place where dreams flourish. I will be there for you in your triumphs and in your disappointments. I pledge myself to you."*

**❧ SPECIAL SETTING** *"How lucky we are to be able to make our pledges to each other in this magnificent outdoor cathedral. We are surrounded by God's handiwork. This place is our inspiration. The mountains give us courage; the trees, a safe haven. May our relationship grow in awareness and responsibility. I want to walk this Earth with you, in peace and harmony."*

❦ SOCIAL CAUSES *"Jane, I offer myself to you as a partner in life. May our compassion for humanity keep us sensitive to needs around us and unite us in love. I am committed to you, and to sharing our love with others through the joyful labor of our hands and hearts."*

❦ SHARED INTERESTS *"I know that ours will be a lifelong commitment of love and faithfulness. Our friendship began when we met as marathon runners. We both understand the discipline required to compete, the personal satisfaction of going the distance. With Isaiah I pray that we will 'run and not be weary, walk and not faint.' I trust you. I love you. I want to be your wife forever."*

# *sharing*

## PRAYER LITANY

Attendants, parents, and special friends each, in turn, read aloud one prayer segment; after each, the congregation responds, *"We give you thanks, O Lord."*

[MAID OF HONOR] *"For your love, freely given, and the love between Jane and John which we are celebrating today,"*

[CONGREGATION] *"We give you thanks, O Lord."*

[BEST MAN] *"For the bonds of friendship and the spirit of unity in this place ..."*

[BRIDE'S MOTHER] *"For families that love and sustain us with joy, comfort, and forgiveness ..."*

[GROOM'S MOTHER] *"For the family of man, the world and all who seek to live in peace ..."*

[BRIDE'S FATHER] *"For all your blessings —this beautiful place, the mystery of love, new beginnings possible each day ..."*

[GROOM'S FATHER] *"For your help in times of need, your promise to support us in illness or other adversity ..."*

[BRIDESMAID] *"For the hope of the future, for our resolve to shape our tomorrows, and for children of tomorrow ..."*

## H Y M N S

- ❖ "Morning Has Broken" [FARJEON]
- ❖ "New Every Morning Is the Love" [WEBBE]
- ❖ "O Perfect Love" [BARNBY]
- ❖ "The King of Love My Shepherd Is" [DYKES]
- ❖ "Joyful, Joyful, We Adore Thee" [VAN DYKE]
- ❖ "Love Divine, All Loves Excelling" [WESLEY]
- ❖ "Now Thank We All Our God" [RINKART]
- ❖ "Praise to the Lord, the Almighty the
  King of Creation" [GESANEUCH]
- ❖ "Blest Be the Ties That Bind" [MASON]

## THE FAMILY MEDA_LION

*Now children of newly blended families can be an inte-
gral part of the ceremony. After the vows, children are*

*called forward to receive promises of
love and inclusion along with a
sterling-silver Family Medallion with
three intersecting circles which symbol-
ize family love.*

✠ *(Above:) To honor children, the Family Medallion.*

# *inspiration*

*I do not wish you joy without a sorrow,*
*Nor endless day without the healing dark,*
*Nor brilliant sun without the restful shadow,*
*Nor tides that never turn against your bark.*
*I wish you love, and strength, and wisdom,*
*And gold enough to help some needy one,*
*I wish you songs, but also blessed silence,*
*And God's sweet peace when every day is done.*
— UNKNOWN

*Love is not love which alters when it alteration finds,*
*Or bends with the remover to remove:*
*O, no! It is an ever fixed mark,*
*That looks on tempests and is never shaken....*
— WILLIAM SHAKESPEARE

*Dawn love is silver, Wait for the west:*
*Old love is gold love — Old love is best.*
— KATHARINE LEE BATES

The fountains mingle with the river
And the rivers with the Ocean,
The winds of heaven mix forever
With a sweet emotion;
Nothing in the world is single;
All things by a law divine
In one spirit meet and mingle,
Why not I with thine?
— PERCY BYSSHE SHELLEY

## LITERATURE

A good marriage, if such there be, rejects the company and conditions of love. It tries to reproduce those of friendship. It is a sweet association in life, full of constancy, trust, and an infinite number of useful and solid services and mutual obligations.

— MONTAIGNE

…I give you my hand!
I give you my love, more precious than money,
I give you myself before preaching or law;
Will you give me yourself? Will you come travel with me?
Shall we stick by each other as long as we live?

— WALT WHITMAN

# MUSIC

Below, songs that may express your feelings during the ceremony or reception.

❖ "Here, There, and Everywhere"

  [LENNON, McCARTNEY]

❖ "A Wedding Prayer" [WILLIAMS]

❖ "The Wedding Song" [STOOKEY]

❖ "Forever and Ever, Amen" [OVERSTREET, SCHLITZ]

❖ "All I Ask of You," Phantom of the Opera

  [WEBBER, RICE]

❖ "Sunrise, Sunset," Fiddler on the Roof

  [HARNICK, BOCK]

❖ "Benedictus" [SIMON AND GARFUNKEL]

❖ "Song of Ruth" [ADLER]

❖ "If We Only Have Love" [BREL]

❖ "This I Find Is Beautiful" [WEISS, DAVID]

❖ "Heart Full of Love," Les Misérables

  [BOUBIL, SCHONBERG, KRETZMER]

❖ "Looking Through the Eyes of Love"

  [BAYER, HAMLISCH]

❖ "The First Time Ever I Saw Your Face" [McCOLL]

❖ "Someone to Watch Over Me" [GERSHWIN]

❖ "Day by Day," Godspell [BERG]

# SCRIPTURE

*"Love is patient and kind; love is not jealous or boastful; it is not arrogant or rude. Love does not insist on its own way; it is not irritable or resentful; it does not rejoice at wrong, but rejoices in the right. Love bears all things, believes all things, hopes all things, endures all things. Love never ends."* — 1 CORINTHIANS 13

*"Two are better off than one, because together they can work more effectively. If one of them falls down, the other can help him up."* — ECCLESIASTES

*"The mountains and hills shall burst into song before you, and all the trees of the field shall applaud."* — SONG OF SONGS

*"Thus saith the Lord; Again there shall be heard in this place ... the voice of joy, and the voice of gladness, the voice of the bridegroom, and the voice of the bride, the voice of them that shall say, Praise the Lord of hosts."* — JEREMIAH

44

# PRAYERS AND BLESSINGS

*"O make these loved companions greatly to rejoice, even as of old art Thou, O Lord, who makest bridegroom and bride to rejoice."*

— ONE OF THE SIX BENEDICTIONS
FROM THE JEWISH WEDDING

*"Now you will feel no rain for each of you will be shelter for the other. Now you will feel no cold for each of you will be warmth for the other. Now there is no more loneliness; now you are two persons but there is only one life before you. Go now to your dwelling —to enter into the days of your life together —and may your days together be good and long upon the earth."*

— APACHE MARRIAGE BLESSING

*"We have decided here and now to marry our son and daughter. Therefore, O goddess of Fire, hearken and be witness. Protect this pair from every illness; watch over them so that they may grow old."*

—TURKO-MONGOLIAN PRAYER

Like everyone in Harmony, Jacob was blind and had been from birth. Everyone born into the community of Harmony Station, along with her sister colonies and mother foundation on Earth, lived without sight.

Stepping out, Jacob reached up and double-tapped his sounder. The pin made its single, bright tone to alert him it was on. Traipsing along, he could feel the warm breeze on his face and smell the fragrance of neighborhood flower gardens. He could hear the voices of people walking by, some laughing, others bickering, most murmuring in quiet tones. He could hear the chords produced by two or more sounders engaging as citizens passed one another or walked together in the street, could hear the single notes sound as some strayed too close to the pathminders. All these sounds flowed together in his mind as he walked, intertwined in a single song that carried him to school.

# TRUESIGHT

# TRUESIGHT

## David Stahler Jr.

*An Imprint of* HarperCollins*Publishers*

Library of Congress Cataloging-in-Publication Data
Stahler, David.
Truesight / David Stahler Jr.— 1st ed.
p. cm.
Summary: In a distant frontier world, thirteen-year-old Jacob is
uncertain of his future in a community that considers blindness a
virtue and "Seers" as aberrations.
ISBN 0-06-052285-2 — ISBN 0-06-052286-0 (lib. bdg.)
ISBN 0-06-052287-9 (pbk.)
[1. Blind—Fiction. 2. People with disabilities—Fiction. 3. Science
fiction.] I. Title.
PZ7.S78246Tr 2004                                      2003011490
[Fic]—dc22

Typography by R.Hult
❖

First paperback edition, 2005
Visit us on the World Wide Web!
www.harpereos.com

*To my wife, Erica*

# PROLOGUE

"There it is."

The floater sped through the early evening along the plains of Nova Campi, rising and falling with the terrain, riding the gentle waves of hills and valleys at an even speed. Clearing a ridge, the two men in the cockpit looked ahead—one with mild interest, the other with open amazement—as the tall sea grasses of the plain parted to reveal a network of fields stretching to the edge of the colony. Large squares of black soil, striped with greens and golds, blues and purples, lay sprinkled with the shapes of men and women bent over the strips of color, pacing slowly up, down, and between the rows with purpose. The floater adjusted to a makeshift road, slowing and lowering closer to the ground.

The two men were computer specialists from the city, from the other colony, from what might as well have been the other side of the world, the other side of the galaxy. Dressed in crisp uniforms, reclining in the shimmering craft, they gazed at the workers in brown smocks who paused in their direction as they passed. The younger technician drove, casually watching the workers as they resumed their chores. He was native to this planet. He had been here before, though not enough times for the sights to become routine. The other, though older, was a newbie, recently shipped to the frontier from older worlds with more established colonies settled by ancient corporations.

"What are they doing?" the newbie asked.

"Farming, agriculture. It's what they do best."

"I know, but I mean, how can they work if they're blind?"

"How should I know? How can they do anything? They just can. They've been doing it their entire lives. They're all blind here in Harmony Station, have been for generations. It's the way they're made—the way they make each other. Christ, didn't you read your colony manual?"

"Look at them turn toward us. It's uncanny, as if they see us but don't."

"Relax. They're only listening. They still have ears, you know. People say their hearing is genetically enhanced, as their blindness is engineered, but I don't believe it. People say a lot of things." He paused, glancing at his partner. "We're coming to the town, so listen—when we arrive, let me do the talking. They're not exactly unfriendly, but they can be touchy."

"How so?"

"Well, they're polite enough, but you get the feeling they really can't stand us. We're just a bunch of Seers to them; they're only Blinders to us. Same old story."

The road—straight, steady—veered toward the settlement, a series of tiered hillsides ringed with streets, punctuated with occasional squares amid squat concrete buildings. In answer to the setting sun, the gleam of metal winked from the tiers—the fronts of homes snuggled into hillsides. The technician eased the floater to a halt at the edge of town, where a half dozen figures stood waiting to receive them. To the newbie, they seemed fairly unremarkable, like any other group of men and women. They wore draping gowns in basic simplicity—no jewelry or headdresses, no images of adornment except for a small broach of gold or silver pinned on each breast. What absorbed him, however, were their eyes. He couldn't stop staring at them—wide open, gazing straight ahead, unmoving, blue green like the strange color of this world's grasses. They seemed to see everything, though he knew they saw nothing. They seemed to see right into his being, to penetrate him with their indifference, like statues of antiquity. He found himself turning his own eyes away, lowering his head, though they certainly could not know he stared.

"Good evening, High Councilor," his partner said.

"Greetings. Jackson, isn't it?" The man in front, his beard long and brown with streaks of gray, his voice gentle, stepped forward as he spoke.

"You remembered."

"Of course. I thought they might send you."

"Councilor, this is my partner, Holman."

"You're new, aren't you? Welcome to Harmony." The councilor bowed in Holman's direction.

"Thanks. Quite a place you have here. Those fields . . . I've never seen anything like them before."

"I suppose I've never seen anything like them before either."

Jackson shot Holman a look. Holman winced and stammered an apology.

"Relax, Holman," the high councilor said. "It was meant to be a joke."

The leader's face passed the slightest smile before returning to blankness. During the entire exchange none of the other residents spoke; they barely moved for that matter. Holman felt a mild urge to bolt, to jump back in the floater and head for civilization, to Melville, the only other colony on this remote planet. Even its small cluster of translucent city towers stretching above the plains and its meager starport—a lightly droning hive with an occasional ship transporting to and from the orbital cruisers like the one that brought him to Nova Campi—were preferable to this place.

"Jackson, tell your partner there is no need to be agitated. We'll soon leave the two of you to your duties."

"How is the ghostbox running? Anything in particular you want us to examine when we do our inspection?"

"The computer has been fine, aside from the usual glitches in our power stream. Nothing we can't tolerate."

"That's right, same problem as last time. We brought a regulator with us. That should help make things somewhat smoother."

"Good. Do you remember the way?"

"Yeah, I can find it. We should be done in a few hours."

"Thank you, Jackson. You can show yourselves out when you've finished, and I'm certain you need no reminders about our rules of contact."

"Not at all. Don't worry, we'll keep to ourselves. Just give us a good review for the bosses, okay?"

"I always do," the councilor murmured as he left. The others followed him, walking slowly, almost symmetrically, down the center of the path. A sullen breeze arose and swished their robes, ushering them away. As they departed, Holman paused. Ever so faintly, he thought he could hear . . . music. Nothing melodic, only the slightest chorus of tones interwoven and shimmering on the breeze. It was simultaneously soothing and unsettling, the soundtrack of a delicate dream.

The sun had nearly vanished; on the horizon it was tiny and pale, its last light thin and obscure. On the opposite horizon, however, the first of Nova Campi's two moons was rising steadily, visibly. Purple and vast, with great rings that glittered at sunset, it seemed to settle and brood over the dusk. It was something, perhaps the only thing, Holman enjoyed about this quiet world. Still, over the last few weeks, he had found himself coming to terms with frontier life. Less and less he missed the continuous dazzle and stimulation of the urbanized worlds closer to Earth.

"Wake up, newbie. Time to work." Jackson interrupted his trance.

"How can they walk so perfectly, so unhindered? It's as if they can see the path."

"They can, in a sense. See those poles that line the walks? Touch one."

"What's it going to do? Shock me?" Holman asked, walking toward the first pole. As he approached, a resistance arose, a mild tingling sensation that was neither painful nor pleasant but simply there, offering greater resistance the closer he got. He moved close enough to touch it, tried extending his hand to grasp the tiny sphere that crowned the rod. His hand shook with the repelling force. It was like trying to join two magnet heads. Impossible.

"Not bad. An invisible fence."

"A corral for everyone."

They skirted the edge of the settlement for several minutes before Jackson steered the two of them to a path, tiled in white stones, stretching to a distant bunker barely visible in the dusk. Holman stopped after only a dozen yards. Something was missing.

"The force poles. There aren't any lining this path."

"I guess they don't need them here," Jackson said. "Or don't want them. There's a lot of sensitive equipment in that building over there."

They continued in silence. It was darker now. The breeze had died, and the grasses, no longer whispering their presence, slipped into the general shadow of the landscape. Only the tiled path, glowing dimly in the faint moonlight, was visible. It penetrated the dusk, dividing the darkness. Jackson stopped and pulled items from his kit. Headlamps. He handed one to Holman. They slipped them around their heads and flipped the switches, flooding each other's faces with light, blinding each other amid sudden apologies. Each turned his gaze away from the other, and soon the world of sight returned to normal, a world reduced to the sphere of illumination their lights provided.

"Jackson, I heard something . . . before. This sounds crazy, but I thought I heard music."

Jackson paused. "Angelic hosts? Don't worry, you're not crazy. Have you noticed the pins?"

"Yeah."

"All the Blinders wear them. I asked about their significance once—their own invention. Each one is tuned to a different frequency, designed to emit a distinct pitch."

"But I didn't hear them at first."

"They usually require a trigger. Like the wands along the street. The closer a Blinder gets, the louder the note. They can also be triggered by another pin; probably so people won't run into one another on the street. They even have a panic function—simply tap it a few times and help is on the way."

"Clever. I wonder if it ever gets annoying, those tones."

"I wouldn't think so. They must be so familiar that they're hardly noticeable, practically subconscious. Still, you never know when it comes to the Blinders.

They might want to annoy themselves for the mere pleasure."

"Pleasure?"

"I don't know. They seem to take a measure of pride in their lifestyle, enjoy wearing a badge of adversity. I guess it can't be that terrible. Everyone seems happy enough, and I've never heard of anyone leaving, or even wanting to. And get this, this is really wild: most of the Blinders are born sightless—you know, prenatal genetic modification—but rumor has it that a few had their eyesight deliberately destroyed and joined the colony as adults. Wackos from Earth, most likely. I mean, would you be blind if you didn't have to be? Holman?"

Holman had stopped and then turned, sweeping his light across the path behind him, then scanning the grass on either side. Jackson followed suit. He saw nothing.

"Mind telling me what we're looking for?"

"Did you just hear something? I thought I heard a rustle."

"I didn't hear anything. You're imagining it."

"In the grass. Clear as day. Someone's out here."

"Nobody's out here, Holman. Look, I realize this place is a bit unusual, especially for someone new to the planet, but relax."

"Something's moving! Look!"

Holman grabbed Jackson's arm, shining his light on a section of grass that flittered and rolled in a wave toward them. Something *was* moving. Jackson's heart began to pound as the wave carried itself to the edge of the path. A shape emerged—white, furry, four legged. It turned and stared at them, its eyes suddenly glowing in the beam of their headlamps.

"A cat?" Holman hissed in disbelief. "A cat? What the hell is a cat doing out here?"

Jackson burst out laughing, relief sounding in his voice. "That's right, I forgot. They have cats. Cats to catch the rats, or whatever it is they call the vermin here. Ugly little critters invade the food supply. The cats love 'em, though."

"How low-tech of them."

Holman had only now released his grip. Still chuckling, Jackson shook his arm to restore circulation. "Hey, it works."

They reached the bunker. The squat steel building at the end of the road was a welcome sight, an island in the darkness. They paused, listening to the low throb of generators that seemed to radiate from the walls. Jackson loved the sound; it was the sound of technology, the sound of power. It was his sound. He smiled and looked at Holman, who stood pale and trembling, his headlamp darting amid the grass.

"Don't feel bad. I reacted the same way when I first visited Harmony—which was only last year, by the way—and I was raised on this planet."

"I don't know. I just feel as if I'm being watched."

"Well, that's probably the only thing definitely *not* happening here. Like I said before, relax."

Jackson removed a slim card from his pocket and ran it through the magnetic slot. A large door slid open before them. As they entered, lights came to life, and the technicians winced momentarily.

"Ah, let there be light," Holman said.

"Probably the only building in the entire colony that's wired for it," Jackson replied.

They switched off their headlamps. Holman smiled as he viewed his surroundings, comforted by the familiar shapes of technology: square and rectangular boxes, colored lights that winked, screens that glowed. Alone, in the center of the room, stood a slender gray obelisk, visually barren in contrast to the gaudy panels that lined the walls. It was the ghostbox, a powerful mainframe that controlled most of the technological functions of the colony. It maintained, it monitored, it diagnosed, it repaired. Though no longer state of the art amid the inner worlds, here at the rim it was a computer demigod. Stately. Beautiful.

"Quite an expensive machine for a place like this; I wonder how they can afford it," Holman remarked.

"Their foundation back on Earth shipped it here a few years ago. A gift from Mommy. C'mon, let's get started. If we hurry, I can be home in time for bed."

"The voice of a newly married man, I'm guessing."

Jackson laughed. "Almost a year. Aren't you married?"

"I was."

"What happened?"

"She didn't like the idea of life on the plains. Hightailed it back to civilization."

They opened their kits and went to work. After a few minutes, Holman spoke again. "Funny, all this equipment here. I mean, these people—farmers, essentially. Self-proclaimed pioneers, self-sufficient, yet how would they live without all this technology? They want nothing to do with the outside world, but they sure seem to depend on it."

"Are you detecting hypocrisy at work?"

"I guess. Don't you think so?"

"I try not to get so philosophical. Besides, they keep us in business."

The next hour passed in total, concentrated silence. Systems were analyzed, programs were checked, stray fragments of data were remerged or cut loose. Holman installed the power regulator. Jackson accessed the ghostbox, programmed the necessary updates. Everything was normal. Everything was fine. They were just finishing up, putting everything back in place, when Jackson turned and saw her.

"Holman."

Holman turned and jumped. She was an apparition, standing at the entrance, pale and delicate, a young woman—almost still a girl—beautiful, with dark hair pulled back tightly and full red lips. She simply stood there, a look of fear on her face despite the eyes that held no focus. Though he didn't believe in superstition, for a moment Holman was sure he was seeing a spirit, a projection of the ghostbox, as if she haunted this place and they were the intruders. Her head suddenly cocked. She became aware of some change. Was it their awareness of her? Holman wondered.

"Who . . . who are you?" Jackson stuttered.

She moved toward him so quickly he retreated in surprise. Her face desperate, she extended a hand, bringing the other one to her face, drawing its index finger to her lips, pleading for silence.

"Be quiet." She whispered so faintly it seemed as though she were only mouthing the words. "They can hear you."

"Who can hear us?" Jackson whispered back.

Suddenly the broach on her chest, a silver swirl, began to emit a light pitch, wavering in rapidly increasing strength. She immediately tapped the pin to deaden the tone and turned to face the door. Holman could hear voices and the sounds of people approaching. He watched her place her arms around Jackson's neck and bring her lips to his ear. He couldn't hear her words, but he saw Jackson's eyes open wide. Before anything else could happen, a group of men entered the room, led by the high councilor. Their broaches toned loudly, suddenly breaking into a pulsing squeal as they entered the room. They, like the girl, tapped the pins. All noise ceased.

"Delaney? Delaney, we know you're in here!" the councilor shouted. No one said a word. Both the technicians and the young woman—everyone in the room, for that matter—became statues. It was as if time had frozen, leaving only the susurrations of the machines to indicate otherwise. The councilor's pin glittered platinum in the light.

"Jackson, give the girl to me." The councilor's voice barely concealed the anger on his face.

"Wait a minute, Councilor. Let's not rush to any conclusions about what's happening here—"

"I'm here, Father," the girl interrupted so suddenly, they all started. She broke away from Jackson and walked toward the men, reaching out her hand until it brushed against the councilor's sleeve. With a sudden jerk, he grabbed her and pulled her to him.

"Take her," he said, handing her off to the two men waiting behind him. They each took a hand and, slowly turning, disappeared into the outer darkness.

"What were you doing with her?" the councilor demanded.

"Honestly, nothing," Jackson replied. His voice was as calm and neutral as the councilor's. "We turned around and there she was. Then you showed up. That's about it."

"What did she say to you?"

"She didn't say anything. There was no time—like I said, you came in right after her. She seemed confused, as if she were lost or something. I don't know."

"Yes, that's probably it. She has been known to wander." The councilor hesitated. Holman sensed he was trying to decide whether or not to believe Jackson. Either he did or he decided it wasn't worth the trouble, because he suddenly spoke again. "Please excuse us."

"No problem. We were just finishing up anyway."

The high councilor left the room. The pair finished their work, packed their kits, and left. Several times Holman had turned to speak, and each time Jackson had shot him a warning glance for silence. They left the bunker quietly and hurried down the path, their headlamps lighting the way. Holman couldn't wait to return to the floater. Each moment the darkness became more oppressive, smothering him. Even the great ringed moon, now far past its zenith and approaching the western horizon, seemed barely to glow in the night. As they topped a rise not far from the floater, they paused once more. This time Jackson grabbed Holman's arm, though not harshly nor in fear. Instead, he pointed to the eastern horizon, where Nova Campi's other, smaller moon now rested, pink and cratered. Silhouetted against it was a dark mass, which Holman realized was a group of figures standing on the hilltop. He turned off his lamp for a moment, though he didn't quite know the reason why. Jackson did the same.

"Listen," Jackson whispered reflexively. Holman could already hear it.

It was music. Not like the chiming tones from earlier in the evening, not like the glistening hums emitted by some mechanical device, but the sound of voices. They were human voices, coming from the singers standing on the hill, intertwined in a choral melody that rose and fell with dynamic intensity, meandering around intricate patterns of melody. The chanters' song contained no words—it needed none, it seemed so ancient. The two technicians stood transfixed until the song concluded. When it ended, they walked in perfect silence back to where the floater glowed pink under the moon.

Not until they were well away from the colony did Holman break the silence.

"That music was incredible. So beautiful," he said.

"Sad, too," Jackson remarked.

Holman didn't think it was sad, but he didn't say so. Instead he asked the question that had been burning in his brain since they left the bunker: "Back there, right before the men came in. What did she say to you?"

Jackson shivered before speaking.

"She said, 'Help me get out.'"

# PART ONE

# CHAPTER ONE

"Ow! You're hurting me!"

"Well, hold still, then."

Jacob squirmed one last time on the stool before settling back down. Snipping scissors sounded in his ear. Always, in the past, the noise had soothed him; the quiet moments he and his mother shared during the monthly shearings had been a constant source of comfort for as long as he could remember. Always, he could feel her hands, delicate and sure, as they caressed his hair, gentle touch reinforced by gentle touch, as hair was cut away. A light pull released by the crisp closure of steel was the rhythm she worked to, a rhythm that worked itself into a lull within him. To this rhythm she would hum in breathy notes the songs of his childhood—the nursery rhymes, the play songs—and the songs of Harmony Station, the songs of its traditions. They rarely talked, and Jacob enjoyed that silence the most; no demands were made, no tests given about rules or history, no pestering inquiries about music or lessons, only touch.

His eyes were closed now against the hairs tickling down over his nose and cheeks. He could sense his mother standing there before him, could smell the essence of the flowers she had been picking from their doorstep an hour ago. Not that it mattered—had his eyes been open, Jacob wouldn't have been able to see her anyway. Like everyone in Harmony, Jacob was blind and had been from birth. Everyone born into the community of Harmony Station, along with her sister colonies and mother foundation on Earth, lived without sight. Jacob himself was hardly aware of what his blindness meant, of what sight meant. The darkness wasn't dark; light, colors, the pictures of the world around him, merely formed an absence that was unaware of itself.

All Jacob knew of the world of sight were the lessons he had learned from his parents and teachers—and from the leaders of Harmony, a council composed of representatives from the Foundation. He knew that sight was a deception, a distraction from the inner world that formed the center of one's being. He understood that vision offered little more than the temptation of appearances or, worse, images of suffering and horror, things that human beings should never have to see.

Though he was taught that sight had its practical advantages on a more mundane level, he had been educated in the history of the Foundation, of how its members had decided long ago to embrace what was once considered a handicap instead of abandoning it to the medical technologies that could make it obsolete. Instead they had decided to make their blindness a way of life, and in accepting the difficulties it yielded, would become stronger in their adversity.

"Ow! You did it again! That's the second time, Ma." Jacob reached up and felt along the ridge of his ear. It burned a little from the poke, but he couldn't feel any blood.

"I'm sorry, but you keep moving. You act as if you have squeaks running up your legs. Care to tell me what's on your mind?"

"No." Jacob shuddered at the thought of the little rodents clinging to his skin. Every three months the native creatures bred in droves that plagued Harmony for at least a week. One of his earliest memories was awakening one night to a swarm of the creatures crawling all over him. He'd screamed, and they had scattered off his back and legs. His parents, terrified, had rushed in to find him sobbing, but otherwise unharmed. They soon located the rodents' source—a mother had built her nest in the narrow space below his mattress and had recently given birth. The next morning they adopted Unger, one of their neighbor's new kittens, who became a competent, if somewhat ambivalent, squeak eater. After that, the problem abated, though for years Jacob relived nightmares of the experience. He still dreamed about them occasionally, though he told his parents he didn't.

"Come on, Jacob. You know you can't hide anything from me. Out with it."

"Nothing is the matter, Ma! Let's just get this over with already."

"Okay. Relax, but remember what you've been learning in school for the past ten years: 'All thoughts are words. All words are shared.'"

*It all depends on the thoughts*, Jacob said to himself. If it concerned something good—like an abundant harvest or a month without lost power—then everyone spoke up. If it was something bad—like when the water systems malfunctioned for a week or neighbors argued—no one wanted to hear it. Only his mother seemed to be the exception, at least with him at home. He could tell his mother was hurt by his reticence, but in a way, Jacob wasn't lying. There really wasn't anything the matter—at least, nothing he could think of specifically. All he knew was that his thirteenth birthday was next week and that school would be finished in a month. Then he would graduate and the harvest would arrive. After that, the future. As occurred for all his classmates, specialization was looming and no one knew what to expect. Soon, though, he and his peers would know what the rest of their lives would entail. It was a broad leap. Perhaps that's what was eating at the edges. Whatever the reason, Jacob was getting sick of the sudden waves of annoyance and frustration that arrived from nowhere and swept over him. He had explained his symptoms to his father, who told him it was called growing up. "That's life. Get used to it," his father had said.

Interrupting his thoughts, Jacob's mother spoke again. "I know what it is. You're nervous about specialization, aren't you? Go ahead, be nervous. Everyone always is anyway, but remember, it's a matter of trust. The council always does what's best for the people."

"But what if I don't like it?"

"Of course you'll like it. Don't talk that way."

"Father didn't. He wanted to be a teacher."

"How do you know that?" she demanded.

"I heard him say it once. One night, when you were arguing."

"Well, he shouldn't have said that—he didn't really mean it. And you shouldn't have been listening. As for that specialization, the Foundation provides most of our teachers directly from Earth. Besides, his performance levels were low, and I don't think he wanted it badly enough anyway. He knows it was for the best, that it was his place to be a grower." She paused, measuring the hair on either side of his head by running it through two fingers from each hand. "That's not to say that having greater responsibility in order to better serve the community isn't a worthy goal."

"Not to mention more food. Better things."

"That's not the way it is around here, Jacob. You know that everyone gets their due."

"Maybe some are due more, then. All I know is that Egan has nicer things than I do, and bigger lunches."

"Your friend's father is an important person."

"So what?"

"I'm almost finished. Just a few more snips." His mother seemed eager to change the subject. Jacob felt the same way. By now his face was itching. He wanted to reach up from under the sheet fastened around his neck and scratch his nose and chin. He decided this would probably be the last haircut from his mother. Egan was already teasing him about it anyway. Soon both of them would stop getting haircuts altogether and join the adult men in the community, either growing their hair long and keeping it pulled back, or shaving it off altogether. Hair grooming was an indulgence for children and for the Seers, who were obsessed with outer appearances and neglected their inner selves.

"Why do you spend so much time trimming?"

"I just want it to be even."

"Why? Nobody can see it anyway."

"Jacob!" She cupped his chin. "You know you're not supposed to speak that way, even at home. Besides," she said, softening, "I'm a musician. You know what kind of perfectionists we are."

"I hope I get a specialization in music," Jacob wished aloud. She didn't answer him.

"Speaking of music," she said, "Delaney will be here soon, and you have classes to attend."

"She's going to officially become your apprentice, right?"

"Of course. She's the most talented student I've taught in years. And the conductors are pushing me to take one on. Guess they think I'm getting old."

"Well, you are."

"Thanks." She traced her hand across his face and tweaked his nose. They both giggled.

"It doesn't hurt that she's the high councilor's daughter, does it?"

"Since when did you become so savvy? No, I suppose it doesn't. But that ultimately isn't important. She's very talented and works hard." She paused. "Still, I'm a little worried about her. She seems distracted lately. Depressed. I'm worried her music will suffer. I spoke to her father about it, and he didn't seem too concerned. Let me know if you hear anything at school. Or if she says anything to you—after all, you practically spend as much time with her as I do."

Jacob was silent. Should he tell her? For the last few days rumors had been whispered around school about Delaney, about her attempt to run away with the Seers. He hadn't had a chance yet to ask her if they were true. He was unsure if he even should—what if she said yes? Right now at least, rumors were just rumors, and he could go on disbelieving. In the meantime he would say nothing to Delaney and especially nothing to his mother. It would only disturb her even more than it had upset him. Delaney was practically a daughter to her, one of the few people besides Jacob that she had warmed to, that she seemed to care about more than her music.

The rumors, the uncertainty, hurt. For in the same way she had become like a daughter to his mother, Delaney was like a sister to him. She even jokingly called him her little brother whenever she saw him. There were many days when Jacob would arrive home from school and Delaney, having just finished her lessons, would stick around, sometimes for hours, as if she were reluctant to go home. He loved those afternoons when they laughed and joked around, or maybe played a duet together on the piano, something light and funny. Sometimes—usually when his mother left to run errands—they would just talk. Or rather she would talk and he would listen to all the wild things she said.

He smiled now, thinking about the time when, in this very room, she had stood up on a chair before him.

"People of Harmony," she began, her voice dropping an octave as she mimicked her father, assuming a tone of mock solemnity, "though I am pleased to announce that power loss was restricted to only four occasions last week instead of the customary five, I have great concerns about the upcoming harvest. It has been brought to my attention by certain members of the community that too many people are laughing and having fun when they should be busier working to help feed our society. Isn't that right, Councilor Donato?"

"Oh yes, High Councilor," she replied to herself, assuming the higher, sycophantic pitch of the woman who represented Jacob's section of the community, "you are right as always!"

"Therefore," she continued, her voice dropping again, "it is the council's decision that, until after the harvest, there shall be no more laughing in Harmony! More picking, less grinning!

"Yes, High Councilor! I quite agree!" she said again in the woman's voice, sending Jacob into peals of laughter so hard he fell off the couch.

"You there," she barked, again taking on the voice of her father, "did you not hear me? Is that laughter I detect? You must be punished for your insubordination!"

She leaped off the chair, pounced on him, and began tickling him all over so that he laughed even harder, all the while begging her to stop. She was laughing now too as she picked him up off the floor and began dancing with him in circles, knocking into furniture as she sang at the top of her voice in wild abandon. Then she left him panting on the couch, banging out an accompaniment on the piano to the song she still sang—a community march, normally slow and proud, now fast and cartoonish under the strains of her voice.

That wasn't the only time she had poked fun at the councilors, especially her own father, and made Jacob laugh with her wicked impersonations. Her boldness awed him. Nor was that all she did. Sometimes she would confess mild transgressions of the rules, and once even wondered aloud what it would be like to see the world with eyes that worked. The fact that she was the high councilor's daughter only made her comments more scandalous, and therefore more captivating.

In this way she reminded him of his best friend, Egan, who was also the child of one of Harmony's leaders. Though Egan never openly questioned the value of the rules or made fun of those in charge, he had a mischievous streak and reveled in stepping out of bounds once in a while—usually trying to drag Jacob with him. He envied the two of them; they were so different from everyone else he knew. Everyone else was like him— passive, respectful, uncomfortable with anything beyond the structure of Truesight, the philosophy that guided their community and their lives. He had always hoped that he could become more like his two friends, that by being around them, their daring might wear off on him. *Maybe someday I'll be different too*, he often thought.

That wasn't to say that he didn't think about things or wonder about life outside Harmony or even question the ways of his community. However, like everyone else, he kept these thoughts to himself and didn't act on them or say them aloud, mostly because he felt guilty for thinking them in the first place. Sure, he had heard people complain before, quietly in private conversations, but no one really dared speak publicly. When they did grumble, it was almost always about minor inconveniences—shortages of certain items or appliances breaking down—certainly never about the leaders of Harmony or their decisions. Maybe that's why he loved the time he spent with Delaney—she said the things he thought, so he didn't have to.

But over the last few months, things had changed. Delaney stayed to visit less frequently, and when she did, her remarks were sharper, her attitude more cynical than usual, sometimes to the point where even he became uncomfortable. At least before he could say it was all just a joke, that it didn't mean anything. Now he wasn't so sure. This change, coupled with the rumor of her attempted escape, bothered him because he couldn't understand it. If anything, her recent displays annoyed him. There seemed to be a certain degree of ingratitude on her part. He couldn't imagine how anyone could think of leaving Harmony, but especially someone like Delaney. She had what Jacob dreamed of having—a specialization in music, a chance to become one of the future premiere performers in the community. Not only that, she was the daughter of the most important person in Harmony, not to mention smart, kind, and talented. Her voice itself was music to his ears. If she couldn't be happy here, what did that say for *his* future?

"There, finished."

"Thanks, Ma. I'll be home by dinner."

"Fine. Laney and I will be working late today;

Harvestsong's approaching. No need to hurry—and Jacob, don't ever tell anyone what you heard your father say. And don't forget to activate your sounder. You already got a warning last week; we can't afford any fines, especially now."

"I will."

Jacob flushed in embarrassment at the memory of the warning. It had been an honest mistake; he had rushed to leave for school and had simply forgotten to turn it on, a normally involuntary gesture. Nothing would've happened if he hadn't bumped into one of the listeners—who rarely activated their own sounders—rounding a corner, a mere block from the school. The memory of the man marching him back to his dwelling, holding his hand tight like a little child, made him cringe. His father had been at home, having just gotten off third shift in the fields. The listener literally handed Jacob to his father, who crushed his hand in anger and embarrassment.

"Your child was found in violation of Harmony's sounder policy," the listener stated coldly. "Please remind him that all citizens must have their sounders engaged in public areas unless specifically instructed otherwise."

"I will."

"This is his first offense, so I will only issue a warning.

Next time, however, you will be fined."

"I understand. Thank you. It won't happen again."

The listener departed. Jacob's father released his grip. Jacob stepped back.

"Good going, Jacob."

"I'm sorry, Dad. I was in a hurry. I forgot, that's all."

"Well, if you forget again and our rations get cut, you're the one who's going hungry, not me."

After the incident he hadn't forgotten, had double-checked each time he entered the street. Just like now. Stepping out, Jacob reached up and double-tapped his sounder. The pin made its single, bright tone to alert him it was on. Traipsing along, he could feel the warm breeze on his face and smell the fragrance of neighborhood flower gardens. He could hear the voices of people walking by, some laughing, others bickering, most murmuring in quiet tones. He could hear the chords produced by two or more sounders engaging as citizens passed one another or walked together in the street, could hear the single notes sound as some strayed too close to the pathminders. All these sounds flowed together in his mind as he walked, intertwined in a single song that carried him to school.

# CHAPTER TWO

Until the last ten minutes, school flowed uneventfully. First session was the usual—citizenship. A mixture of history and civics, citizenship taught students about the origins of the Foundation, about the settlement of the rim worlds and the founding of their own colony of Harmony Station. Over the past week, as school drew to a close, Jacob and his fellow students had presented final projects. Each student was assigned a topic and was required to speak before the class. Jacob had hoped for a topic about the importance of music in the Foundation—he could easily have put something together. He already knew a lot about it from his mother and had listened to many stories on the subject from recordings in the school library. Maybe that's why his teacher didn't assign it to him.

Instead he was given a history topic—the formation of the original community, which led to the

Foundation's establishment. Still, the project wasn't that difficult. He and his classmates knew much of the information already. The presentations were more or less recapitulations of the material they had been hearing continually since starting school ten years ago. Their teacher said it was important at the end of their education to bring it all together and commit it to memory. That way it would remain with them always and provide a sense of purpose and community. Jacob understood all that. He was already proud of Harmony and its sister colonies, despite Delaney's jokes and his own questions. He especially admired the first founders, a gathering of blind couples early in the twenty-first century, when bioengineering was first becoming standard practice among expectant parents back on Earth, who decided that their children would be born like them. In Jacob's mind, in all their minds, these couples were pioneers, braving the criticisms of others, of Seers who misunderstood and judged them cruel. What the Seers failed to comprehend, what Jacob and his classmates knew, was that experience was relative. What one person or group thought was important or true wasn't necessarily so.

Jacob had to admit, it was interesting reviewing their lessons on the initial community of the blind. What he didn't understand was why they never really learned anything else about the rest of the world. They were taught little about the Seers. Most of their learning involved the many wars that had occurred among the nations on Earth and later among the corporations in space. Continual battles over territory and trading rights, atrocities committed by one organization against another, betrayals and subterfuge—an enormous catalogue of sin.

Once he'd asked his teacher about the Seers. "They can't all be that bad, Mrs. Lawson. Can they?"

For a moment silence filled the air. Nobody seemed to breathe. They all waited for the answer.

When Mrs. Lawson spoke, her voice was calm but cold. "No, Jacob. You're correct. They're not all that bad. But even the best of them are limited by their arrogance, by their search for ease in life, by their obsession with material things. They think they know the answers, but in their own way they are the ones who are truly blind."

That was one of the few times, and the last, that Jacob had asked a question. In general, questions were not asked or encouraged. When someone asked one on a rare occasion, that student was usually met with a perfunctory response: "That's not important right now," or "We'll cover that later," or "You don't need to know that."

Yes, Jacob enjoyed history; it was the other aspect of citizenship class that he didn't care for—what Mrs. Lawson called civics, mostly comprised of constant drills in the rituals and rules of the community. It seemed like there were regulations for everything. Where people could go and when. What they could do, who they could talk to, and where. It wasn't that he didn't think it was important; obviously it was—as his recent warning from the listener had reminded him. It was just that it was boring. Over and over again they repeated the same rules, repeated the proper words to speak at the Gatherings, sang the same songs. It was nothing new. They knew all the rules and songs, which their parents had ingrained in them from the time they could utter their first words. They had been attending the weekly Gatherings for just as long. Jacob didn't complain outwardly, though. No one did. It wasn't the way of the community.

Second session was more interesting. The topics varied, depending on the day of the week. Some days it was music, which Jacob loved most of all. Other days it was science, mostly learning about different kinds of plants, their medicinal and nutritional qualities, their growth cycles, and basic genetics. Today they studied orienteering, the essentials of managing in a sightless world. Having spent their entire lives in Harmony, they all had a clear sense of the layout of the community already. Still, they learned many particulars that Jacob liked for their practicality. They learned how to perform household duties, like cooking and cleaning. They learned how to work in a crop and what to do when lost. Their lessons emphasized safety and efficiency.

Jacob also liked orienteering because they played games, such as seeker, a more sophisticated form of hide-and-seek they had been playing since early childhood. They would have team adventures in which they were brought to an unknown area and competed in finding their way back to school. Jacob was amazed at how much he had learned in the past few years, how much more confident he felt moving around the house and around the streets of Harmony on his own. He loved the freedom the knowledge brought him. He loved how in the past two years his parents had allowed him to leave the house alone, no longer having to be accompanied, always holding one of their hands.

Jacob and his classmates also studied technology. Some days they were taught how their sounders worked, or how the pathminders kept them from walking off the streets. Once they were even taken to the computer. Jacob could still remember the hum that permeated the cool chamber. They learned about what Mr. Robison—their orientation teacher—called the ghostbox, the machine that helped Harmony in so many ways, doing everything from serving as community surgeon to processing the food they grew.

Today they were being taught to use a new gadget, a device called a finder. Jacob had heard of it but had never used one, let alone handled one. He and Egan had been waiting all week for this.

"Please remember," Mr. Robison said, distributing several of the devices, "these are expensive instruments. Most of you will never need to use one, but you should learn in case of an emergency."

"Who does use them?" a classmate asked. Unlike Mrs. Lawson in citizenship class, and many of Jacob's other teachers, Mr. Robison didn't mind questions. He actually seemed to like them.

"Well, Fiona, mostly the listeners because they have the burden of protecting us, making sure we follow the rules so we don't hurt ourselves or others. Also, the guardians in the fields use them so they can better manage the growers."

"What do finders do?" asked another student.

Egan, sitting next to Jacob, snorted quietly in disdain. Jacob felt the same way. Everyone knew what a finder was for.

"Egan Spencer—I heard that. Impoliteness is unacceptable. Apologize to Angus."

"I'm sorry, Angus," Egan said flatly.

"I meant, how do they work?" Angus said resentfully.

"I know you did," Mr. Robison reassured him. "Jacob, why don't you and Beth come up here."

Jacob arose from his seat and walked to the front of the class, trailing his fingertips along the right-hand row of desks as he passed. He could hear Bethany do the same, could sense her near him as they approached each other. He inhaled deeply as she moved close to him. She smelled of lilacs. She always smelled of lilacs. Her mother was a scentmaker who grew her own flowers, using them in the soaps and perfumes that made her a popular figure in Harmony.

"A finder is actually easy to use. It's really just a tiny but powerful computer that holds in its memory a perfect map of Harmony, much like you retain at this point in your own minds. It also contains a sensor that can register any person's sounder, and its range is practically unlimited. The listeners could locate you just about anywhere on the planet, I'd imagine—not that they would ever need to. You hold the finder in your hand, point it straight in front of you, speak the person's name into the device, and slowly begin to rotate. You can set the finder to emit a light tone or a silent pulse. For now we'll use the tone. Beth, leave the classroom and stand out in the hall. Walk a few yards in whatever direction you wish, so that you're around the corner."

As Jacob heard her walk out, a small cylinder was placed in his hands. It was relatively short with two buttons near the tip.

"Beth, you can still hear me, can't you?"

"Yes, Mr. Robison."

"Good. Class, two buttons are mounted on the device. The right-hand one alternates between tone and pulse. The left-hand button records. Hold it down as you say the name. Go ahead, Jacob."

Jacob pushed down the left button and said, "Bethany Tyler." Immediately a low beep began to emanate from the finder in his hand.

"Okay, now slowly turn in what you think is the right direction."

Jacob turned left and the beep quickened, rising slightly in pitch.

"Good. Now, Jacob, walk in the direction you think the finder is telling you to go and bring Beth back in here."

Jacob located the point of the sound's greatest intensity and slowly walked in that direction. When the beep slowed or lowered in tone, he stopped to take another reading. Soon he could sense himself out in the hallway. He turned right, in the direction of the lilac scent. The beeping rose frantically in pitch, accelerated until it was nearly a continuous stream of sound. He reached out and felt the smooth skin of her arm, traced his hand down to her hand. Their fingers interlocked. Her hand felt warm, soft.

"Hi, Jacob," she whispered.

"Hi" was all he could manage. Holding hands, they walked back into the room. They rejoined Mr. Robison in front, finally releasing their hold.

"How was it, Jacob?" Mr. Robison asked.

"Fine," he said, hoping the nonchalance of his words might hide the quiver in his voice. "I mean, it was easy."

"All right. You two can return to your seats."

Jacob went to give the finder back to his teacher.

"No, you keep it for now. All right, I want everyone to select a partner. Each pair will be given a finder for practice outside. Once you have a partner and a finder, meet at the fountain in the yard."

As always, Jacob and Egan paired up and walked outside. Soon everyone was gathered by the fountain. For the remainder of the session, they practiced using the finders, taking turns hiding and locating each other. They practiced in silent mode. Jacob found it strange at first to feel the pulsing waves passing from the cylinder into his hand, increasing in speed and intensity as he locked onto and moved toward Egan. Before long it became second nature, almost reassuring to be led with such precision, trusting the senses of the machine.

Class was almost over. Jacob was standing quietly, hiding around the corner of the school, waiting for Egan to come to him with the finder, when the pain began. It started as a dull ache in the back of his head. A wave of nausea swept over him. He reached out and gripped the wall, struggled to remain standing. Soon, however, the pain sharpened as it spread out and around him, a web of fire lacing through his skull and gathering at the front into a cluster that threatened to burst from his forehead. Then, fading like an echo, it disappeared, and he was left shaking. A hand brushed his shoulder and took hold of his arm.

"Jacob! Hey, Jake." It was Egan, shaking him. "I found you. Come on! What's going on? You all right?"

"I don't know. I had a headache, all of a sudden."

"Aw. Maybe little Jakey needs to go home and take a nap."

"Funny. Give me the finder, it's my turn."

"Too late. Time's up. Besides, you're not feeling good, remember?"

"No, I'm okay." It was true; he was feeling better.

"Good. Anyway, Mr. Robison says it's time to go. Told us to put the finders in his desk."

They walked side by side back to class. But before going in, Egan grabbed Jacob gently by the arm and pulled him aside. He placed his hand over Jacob's mouth to signal quiet. Jacob felt uneasy. Such a gesture was considered antisocial and rude. There was even a rule against it. To be silent, either alone or with another, for the express purpose of preventing your fellow citizens from knowing your whereabouts went against the spirit of Harmony.

When the others had gone inside, Egan removed his hand and whispered, "Come on, let's keep it."

"Keep what? The finder?"

"That's right. Take it home with you."

"Yeah, right. Do you know what would happen if Robison noticed it was missing?"

"He'll never notice. We'll fool around with it tonight and return it tomorrow."

Jacob paused. Egan waited for him to give in as usual.

"I can't, Egan. I just got a warning last week for not having my sounder on. If I get in trouble again, that's it."

"Don't be a coward, Jacob."

"Why don't you take it home, then? Your father's a councilor. You never get in trouble."

"No. Forget it. If you're not into it, it's not worth it.

When are you going to relax and take some chances once in a while?"

"I've got to go. Put the finder back, okay, Egan?"

"Yeah, all right."

"Thanks," Jacob said, but Egan had already disappeared.

# CHAPTER THREE

All the way home Jacob thought about his odd experience during the finder session. The headache was unlike any he had suffered before—so violent and sudden. Should he tell someone? He couldn't imagine telling his father, who never wanted to hear anything, especially a complaint. He should probably confide in his mother, but she was already worried about Delaney. Would he have to go to the doctor? Be examined by the ghostbox? Maybe he had imagined the entire episode. It had merely been a bad headache, like the migraines Egan's mother endured from time to time.

Before long he arrived home. So absorbed in thought, he almost missed the turn into his yard, would have missed it had his sounder not buzzed suddenly, matching notes with a familiar pitch that grew louder until their hands clasped.

"Hi, Delaney." Jacob tried to sound as upbeat as he

could to avoid revealing in his voice what he now harbored in his mind.

"Hey, Jacob." Delaney sounded flat, tired. Still holding his hand, she pulled him down to sit beside her on the step, putting her arm around him to draw him in the way she always did. The familiarity of the gesture comforted him. Maybe—in spite of her tenor, in spite of the rumors—things weren't so bad.

"How were your lessons? Hope Mother went easy on you today."

"She was fine. I wasn't the best pupil today, however."

"You don't sound too good. Are you sick?"

"Yes, I am sick. Sick of things. Sick of people."

Jacob stiffened at her remark. "Are you sick of me? Of Mother?" he asked softly, pulling away. He didn't know what else to say. The way she spoke made *him* sick. He had never heard her sound this critical, even in the last few months. He had never heard anyone sound so dejected. It scared him. A hand caressed his face.

"'Course not. Don't talk like that. Regina is always kind, and you're my little brother. Remember that."

Her voice had softened, but her words failed to comfort him. The bitterness was gone, but she spoke with a sadness now that somehow seemed far worse.

"Then what's the matter?" It embarrassed him to

hear his voice tremble so, to sound so small and far away.

"Don't you ever wonder what's out there, beyond these streets, beyond the fields?"

"No." It wasn't true; he had wondered. But he didn't want to encourage her—he only wanted her to stop talking like this.

"I do."

*Uh-oh*, Jacob thought, *here we go*. "You're just going through a tough time right now. It'll pass," he said, trying to sound grown up and strong.

She laughed. "You too, huh? You sound just like my father."

"Well, maybe he's right."

She didn't answer. A minute passed, the silence building until, unable to avoid the question in his mind, he blurted out at last, "Are you going to run away again?"

"You heard?" she snorted. "Of course you'd hear. Everybody knows everyone else's life around here, probably better than they know their own. That's what my *father* says, anyway."

"I heard some kids talking in school, but I didn't believe it."

"'Course not," she said. Her voice now slipped low, mimicking her father as she had done so often for Jacob in the past. "No one has ever left Harmony before. No one has ever wanted to." Her impression was savagely perfect, but this time Jacob didn't laugh.

"Mother doesn't know."

"She'll find out. If you don't tell her, someone else will."

Jacob didn't know how to respond. He felt as if there were something he had to say or ask, like the words of a magic spell that would solve everything. Make everything good again. Magic words that could heal Delaney, take away the sickness. All he could do was repeat himself.

"Are you going to run away again?"

She reached down and, cupping his face in her hands, kissed him on the forehead.

"Don't worry about me, Jacob. It's not right that you should, or that I should trouble you."

*You can trouble me*, he wanted to tell her. He regretted his earlier annoyance at her defiance. He had been selfish to be irritated by her pain.

She released him entirely and stepped down into the street.

"I've got to get home. Father's been a little strict lately about my comings and goings. You can guess the reason why. I practically had to threaten him not to send a bodyguard along—to protect me, of course, mostly from myself. Bye, Jacob. We'll talk later."

And then she was gone. Jacob lingered in the yard, listening to her footsteps fade, thinking about her words and the question she had left unanswered.

"Jacob, what are you doing out here?"

Jacob started. It was his mother. He felt as if he had been caught doing something terrible. Maybe he had been.

"Are you all right? Come in for supper."

Without a word, he turned and walked past his mother.


"Is there any more?" Jacob asked, finishing his plate of mashed turnip and greens, swallowing the last of his bread.

"I'm sorry, Jacob. That's it," his mother said. "Didn't you have enough?"

"No, that's okay. I'm full," he lied. Lately food supplies were running low in Harmony. Last year had been a poorer harvest than expected. On top of that, the cattle—the colony's main source of meat and dairy—had contracted some native strain of virus, and many had died before the computer could diagnose and treat with the proper antibodies. As a result, rations had been reduced. Some in the colony grumbled, but none openly complained. They understood the necessity of rationing. Besides, no one was actually starving; there was sufficient food that the council deemed it unnecessary to import more from the outside or bargain with the Seers. Still, at times Jacob felt like he could eat more. A lot more. His mother said he was growing. He suspected she was giving him some of her share behind her husband's back, but Jacob couldn't prove it.

"No one needs to worry," his father explained. "Harvest is almost ready and we're on track for a record yield. Those new fertilizers we developed did the trick. Everyone's rations will return to normal. I also heard," he said, dropping his fork on the table to signal he was done, "we're getting a new shipment of cattle. Straight from Earth. From the Foundation. They've produced a more disease-resistant strain, I guess."

"It's okay, Dad. I'm not hungry."

"Well, I am, and I have to say, despite your mother's ingenious recipes, I'm getting a little tired of turnips. Not that the turnip isn't a wonderful vegetable"—Jacob's father paused for effect—"right, Jacob?"

Jacob's mother laughed at the joke. Since early childhood Jacob had hated turnip, and for a long time had refused to eat it. Not these days.

"What's wrong, Jacob? Too old to laugh at my jokes anymore?" Jacob was silent. "He's so serious, Gina."

Jacob knew his father was trying to draw him out. Referring to him in the third person to his mother always made him speak up.

"You have been a bit quiet since you got home." His mother reached out to touch his arm. "Did something happen at school today?"

Jacob didn't know how to respond. He couldn't tell them the truth, but he didn't want to lie, not about this. "We learned to use finders today—it was interesting. Ma, how were your lessons with Delaney?"

"Did you run into her on her way out? Thought I heard you two talking out there."

"Yeah. She seemed like she wasn't feeling good."

"That's what I thought too. Today was terrible. She couldn't focus; her timing was way off. She even broke down crying at one point. I just backed off—it happens to everyone. It even used to happen to me when I was her age. Still, this has been going on for too many days now. Did you hear anything at school, Jacob? Like we talked about this morning?"

What should he say? He hated to tell on Delaney, but it almost seemed like she wanted him to tell his mother. Maybe it would sound better coming from him.

"Actually, Ma, I did hear something."

"Well, what? Tell me." She seemed eager, but frightened.

"A couple of the kids said she tried to run away."

"What?" He could hear the shock straining her voice as she cried out. She paused to collect herself. "That's impossible. I would've heard that. She would've told me." Jacob was nervous. His mother was upset. "When did she supposedly try it?"

"Last week. I guess a couple of men from the outside came in. She tried to leave with them."

"What were Seers doing here?" she wondered.

"They were probably just some technicians from Melville," his father replied. "They have to be brought in from time to time. Don't be upset, Gina. She's just going through a spell."

"Richard, I should be upset about this. And so should you." Her voice sharpened. "Did you know about this already?"

"I had heard something about it from Anders a couple days ago. I didn't think I should tell you."

"Jacob, go to bed." *Uh-oh*. He knew that sound in his mother's voice. There was going to be a fight. She pulled him to her as he arose. She ran her hands through his hair, inspecting her morning's work, and kissed him on the cheek. "Now go," she said. For once he didn't protest. It had been a long day. He was exhausted.

As soon as he closed his door, he could hear the

voices rise. The thick door muffled the words, but he could sense what they were saying from the inflections, the mostly hostile inflections, in their voices. He undressed and fell onto the bed. Reaching up, he took down the music box from his bureau and held the tiny cube. The metal toy felt cool and smooth, heavy in his hand. He had received it as a gift on his fifth birthday. *Eight years ago next week*, he thought. For almost three years he had played the tune every night while falling asleep. Since then, he played it only when they fought. Things had been quiet lately; he hadn't listened to it in a while.

Now he wound the handle, spun it a dozen times, and let it play. The tiny notes plucked in his ear a melody he had learned long ago, the melody all of Harmony's children learned. It was a child's song, about a woman who planted some flower seeds that sprouted into little boys and girls. She watered the seeds, and they grew in the sun, stayed rooted in the earth, and never got picked. He could still remember the words of the refrain:

> *The maiden came and planted them;*
> *The soil holds them safely.*
> *They don't need eyes to love the sun,*
> *Or flourish in its beauty.*

He couldn't recollect the rest of the lyrics, but it didn't matter. It was the melody he loved. Simple. Pure. The box played its song with mechanical precision. As Jacob listened more intensely, he realized something for the first time. It wasn't just the melody that soothed him. Even more than the song, he found he loved the hum that carried underneath, the sound of the little motor as it unwound itself, steadily slowing to a stop. It was the hum he now heard beyond any other sound, even the song of the music box itself. It was the motor's hum that carried him off to sleep.

# CHAPTER FOUR

The notes resonated from the piano, rising and falling about him, absorbing every worry, driving away all thinking until they became his only thought, a consciousness of sound. He had run through the piece at least fifteen times in the last hour, struggling to get it right, to make it perfect the way it should be, the way it deserved to be. And now he had almost done it. He was nearly to the end. For months he had been working to master his favorite piece, Chopin's Nocturne in E-flat major, and now . . . he had finally done it. He let the final chord ring, luxuriating in the sustained waver of joy.

"You were a little fast on the crescendo in the sixth measure," his mother said casually, coming out of the bedroom where Jacob thought she'd been napping.

"Thanks," he snapped, clapping the cover down over the keys. She came up behind him and ran her fingers across his hair. *Probably checking her haircut again*, he thought. She kissed him on the head.

"Don't be upset," she said. "You almost had it."

"You never encourage me," he muttered.

"I'm sorry, sweetie. You played it beautifully, and with feeling."

"That's not what I mean. You know I want to be a musician—like you and Delaney."

She sat down beside him now on the bench. He could hear the hesitancy in her voice as she spoke.

"Jacob, I love that you love music, that it means so much to you. No matter what happens in the future, it will always be a part of your life."

"So you don't think they'll choose me for a music specialization?" He felt a sinking feeling down in his stomach. What did she know?

"That's not what I'm saying, Jacob. I don't know what they're going to decide."

"But you must have some say. . . ."

"Not really. You would think I do, but I don't. All I'm saying, sweetie, is that I don't want you to be disappointed if you don't get the choice you want. Being a musician is a tough specialization. It takes a lot of hard work and skill. You are a good player, Jacob, but it may not be your greatest talent. Who knows? Maybe the council has something even better in store for you. The high councilor has mentioned to me on more than one occasion how well you do in school, how highly your teachers speak of you."

"So you don't think I have what it takes."

"I think you're a smart, sensitive, and obedient boy, the way I raised you to be. I know that no matter what happens, you'll do something special. You *are* special."

"Thanks," he mumbled. He slid around and stood up from the bench.

"Jacob, do me a favor—run over to the Corrows' and tell Delaney that I have to reschedule tomorrow's lesson. The caller's on the blink again. I forgot to tell her I have to play at a luncheon in the South Tier tomorrow. Besides, you haven't been out of the house today. Be good for you to get some air."

"Fine," he said. After this conversation he was eager enough to leave the house anyway.

"Don't stay too long," she called out as he opened the front door. "There's a Gathering tonight, in a couple hours, and I want you to come with me."

"Okay."

"And Jacob," she called out again. She waited, as if unsure he still remained.

"Yes?" he said, pausing in the threshold.

"Say hello to Delaney's father for me."

"Right." He closed the door and left.

* * *

Jacob walked through the streets in silence, ignoring the greetings of passersby. The antisocial gesture was a violation of the rules, but compared with everything else right now, it wasn't a major concern. Rubbing his forehead, he even forgot for the moment what his mother had said. Last night, for the third time since the initial attack in the school yard, he had awoken to pain. The first two headaches had roused him from sleep but had been less severe than the one at school. He didn't have any headaches at all for three nights after that and assumed that whatever caused them had disappeared. He had almost forgotten all about them until last night, when he suddenly found himself awake in bed, convulsing from a pain so severe he could only whimper through clenched teeth. Its intensity, far greater and longer lasting than the initial attack, frightened him. Even now the memory of it seemed to linger on his brow as his fingers pushed back along the skin of his forehead, as if he could rub it away for good.

He turned in to the home of the high councilor and passed up the ramp that led to their door. Theirs was not a simple hillhouse like the others in the colony, but a stone bunker, large and square, not far from the council chamber in the heart of the community. Going to knock, he realized the door was open. He could hear muffled voices coming from inside. Without thinking, he passed into the entryway and started down the hall that led to the living room, from where the voices seemed to come. As he got closer, though, he suddenly realized the tone of the conversation sounded angry. He paused in the hallway, not sure what to do. He felt guilty for listening—eavesdropping was a major offense—but something compelled him to stay, to move in closer to the doorway until he could hear what was being said. He could perceive the sharp voice of Delaney but couldn't quite make out her words. He moved closer still.

"No one leaves Harmony," said the deep voice of the high councilor. "No one's ever left." There was a pause. "Why do you want to leave, Delaney? You have everything here. People who love you, a promising career. You know what's out there? Nothing. Garbage, violence, hate, shallow people leading shallow lives, never knowing their depths."

"How do you know? You've never been outside Harmony; you've hardly spoken to anyone except the few who have to come here. You don't know a single Seer, I mean really know any one of them. All you know is what you've been told. That's all anyone here knows. It's us versus them. Right? Blind or not, it's pretty easy that way."

"And you? You know nothing. How do you know it's *not* that way? Why risk what you have, what I've given you?"

"You're right. I don't know about the world out there. But I want to find out for myself."

Jacob could hear the councilor wait, resisting her defiance. When he spoke again, his voice sounded gentler. "Come now, Delaney. There's something else behind all this. Tell me the truth. I suppose it's my fault, right? I'm too harsh. I'm mean, as you used to tell me. On the contrary—if anything, I've spoiled you. So why do you want to run away from me?" She didn't answer. "Delaney, I don't like saying this, but you're ill. You're depressed, desperate. We'll take care of you. Maybe the ghostbox can help you, prescribe something so you'll feel better. You're sick, Delaney, that's all."

"Stop telling me what I am." She was crying now. Jacob could hear her sobbing quietly. After a moment she whispered, "Father, I want to see."

Jacob heard a slap, heard Delaney cry out. The sounds stirred him from where he stood transfixed in the hall. In a panic he turned and fled down the hallway, out through the door, running as quietly as he could, trying not to give himself away, trying to forget what he'd just heard. Which was worse—Delaney's shocking admission or her father's reaction? He wanted to keep on running, but he stopped in the dooryard. He still had to deliver his message. Besides, his interruption would stop the fight, wouldn't it? For now, at least.

He returned to the door, closed it, and knocked loudly. When the door opened a moment later, the proximity of their sounders set his to ringing against Delaney's.

"Jacob," she cried. She sounded relieved.

"Who is it?" her father called out from the hallway behind her.

"Jacob Manford," she snapped back.

"Jacob!" the high councilor said. His voice had completely changed, returning to its normal smooth sincerity. There was no sign of anger. "Come in, young man."

Jacob stepped back into the hall for the second time. Delaney reached out and pulled him to her, draping her arms over his shoulders so that he stood between her and her father.

"What brings you here, son?" the man asked.

"Yes, what brings you to our happy home?" Delaney added sarcastically. Jacob could feel the tension hanging in the air.

"My mother sent me over to tell you, Delaney, that she has to cancel tomorrow's lesson."

"Great!" said Delaney with mock enthusiasm. "I have a lot of other work to do tomorrow anyway. Don't I, Father?"

The high councilor chuckled nervously. "Don't be silly, Delaney. I'm sure you've got plenty of practicing you can do on your own."

"Oh really? Is that what you want?" she retorted. From behind him, Jacob could feel the rising intensity of her voice.

"Is everything okay?" Jacob asked tentatively.

"Of course. Of course it is," the high councilor broke in. "Don't mind her, Jacob. She's just in one of her moods today. Everything's fine."

"Oh yes. Everything's fine," she mocked. "As if anything could possibly be wrong in Harmony. In sweet, sweet Harmony—"

"Enough!" The high councilor's roar startled all of them. For a moment no one spoke. Finally Martin Corrow laughed again. "I'm sorry, Jacob. You've caught us on a bad day. If you'll excuse me, I have to go prepare for the Gathering. Delaney, I'll return shortly. I'll expect you to be ready."

When he had left, Delaney grabbed Jacob and headed outdoors.

"Where are we going?" Jacob asked as they walked along the street. She was leading him by the hand, nearly pulling him as she marched along with a rapid stride, so that he had to trot to keep up.

"Nowhere, apparently," she replied. "I just need to get out of that house for a minute," she added, slowing her pace.

"He seemed mad."

"Oh, he's mad, all right. He's always mad," she snorted.

"He's never seemed that way before to me," Jacob offered. He didn't know why, but he felt the need to rationalize the high councilor's anger. "He seems to really care about you."

She suddenly stopped, and he bumped up against her. "About me? I'm an embarrassment, that's what I am. He cares about how things seem. That's all that really matters to him. There's a lot about him you don't know, Jacob."

Maybe that was true, but he didn't want to hear it now. A bell sounded from the square not far away. It rang three times, signaling one hour to the Gathering. The afternoon was coming to an end—Jacob could feel a cooler breeze coming in off the plain and the birds began their evening song. He suddenly felt tired.

"Can't we just pretend everything's okay? Like it used to be? We used to have fun. Just for now, let's pretend," he pleaded.

He could sense her hesitation. Then she sighed and squeezed his hand. "All right," she said. "I'll pretend. For you."

She squeezed his hand again, and they turned around and headed back to her house. They took their time, walking slowly, deliberately. But though they were together, though he could feel the warmth of her hand, the beating of her pulse within his hand, she seemed more distant than ever, withdrawn into her silence, both further in and farther away.

They had reached her yard again. She took a step toward the house but still held his hand.

"I better go in," she said.

"Okay."

She let go her grip, and he let his hand drop, but neither of them moved.

"I don't know," she said slowly. "Maybe he's right about me. Maybe I am just depressed. Sick."

"Of course you're not. Don't say that."

She didn't reply at first. For a moment neither of them spoke. When she did speak again, her voice was quieter, and he could tell her back was to him.

"Thanks, Jacob," she said. He listened to her steps all the way up the ramp, listened to the door open and close. Only then did he turn to go.

* * *

"Come on, Jacob! We'll be late for the Gathering."

"Here I am, Ma. I'm ready," Jacob said, coming into the kitchen. His mother took his hand and they left the house. "Where's Dad?" he said as they entered the street. It wasn't unusual that he had missed dinner, but they always attended Gatherings as a family.

"In the fields."

"Still? Nobody works during a Gathering."

"He said his shift would probably have to go a little late. They've got a lot of preparations to make for harvest. Don't worry, he'll be there."

They were walking for less than a minute when his mother suddenly stopped and drew him aside. He could feel her breath as she leaned down to his ear.

"Jacob," his mother whispered, "you forgot to activate your sounder again." She reached over and tapped the pin on his chest. He suddenly realized that he had been silent, that only his mother's note, a perfect high C, was quivering in the air. His D-sharp in a lower register sounded subdued and quiet as their tones mingled. He could hear other notes begin to chime as they came up behind a crowd, and they all moved toward the central square where every Gathering was held. He felt annoyed at having forgotten again. On the other hand, he was still rattled by the scene at Delaney's house. The words of her upsetting admission to her father continued to echo in his memory as they had all the way home. She had joked about seeing once or twice in the past to Jacob, had wondered what it would be like, but this was different. Jacob shivered now, remembering her voice in the house barely an hour ago as she confessed her desire. It was devoid of humor, of even her characteristic defiance—an utterance of quiet desperation.

They turned onto a wider street. No one spoke. All that could be heard was the chord of sounders woven together, growing louder as more and more citizens merged into the broad avenue that led to the square, until even the muffled steps of shoes scuffing the stones beneath their feet were lost in the music.

They were in the square now. Jacob could no longer feel the mild resistance of the pathminders to his right. Instead he felt the touch of hands from the crowd around him on his back, shoulders, and arms. He, in turn, reached before him to touch the back of another in front. He wondered who it was. Could it be one of his teachers? A neighbor? His own father? Maybe it was Beth. Maybe it was a stranger. His mother held his left hand and they pressed forward, moving deeper into the square, into the mass of bodies. Now the combined sounders of virtually everyone in the colony blended into a single chord of myriad notes, rising to a fevered intensity, creating overtones that seemed to hover in the air above them like insects.

This part of the Gathering Jacob had always loved. He found comfort in the anonymous bodies of those around him, in the loss of self that accompanied his own anonymity. He liked being part of something bigger than himself, adding his own sound to the music of the hive. But today the single sustained chord overwhelmed him; it sounded dissonant and oppressive in his ears, and the bodies around him seemed to be smothering him. The realization crept up on him slowly, a deep and hidden awareness that flirted beneath his consciousness before bursting to the surface. Now his anonymity terrified him, as if he were slipping away from himself, losing himself within the single mass that surrounded him like the grasses of the plain. He felt trapped and had to fight the urge to bolt, had to resist the waves of nausea that were rising at the corners of his consciousness.

Again, as last night, a wave of pain overtook him and he stiffened, bracing himself as the sounders shrieked around him. They pierced his eardrums with their quavering overtones. Now the pain became localized, erupting from its deepest recesses into his eyes.

He gasped at its intensity and closed his lids against the pins that pierced the delicate membrane of his eyeballs. Closing them seemed to offer relief, as if someone had poured water on the fire in his brow.

"Ow, Jacob, you're hurting me." His mother was yelling in his ear, though she was barely audible against the sounders. She was trying to pull her hand away from his grasp, and he realized he had been gripping her so tightly that his hand was beginning to cramp and his nails were digging into her knuckles. He relaxed his grip and swallowed. His mouth was dry and had a sour taste. He had to be careful of her hands—she was a musician, her hands were precious. A cymbal crashed and then crashed again. The signal for silence. Simultaneously hands touched sounders, and the chord abruptly ceased. Jacob breathed a sigh of relief. The silence relaxed him, and the impulse to flee receded.

"Welcome, citizens of Harmony!" a man said into the silence. It was the high councilor. His voice surrounded them, amplified by speakers that bordered the square. Jacob listened to the voice that only a few hours ago had been fuming with rage. It was hard to believe it was the same. This voice was the normal voice, the one he'd heard the second time he went into the hallway, the one he'd always heard before. He suddenly realized there was no differentiation in tone between the voice that had spoken to him then and the one that spoke now to a crowd of several hundred. In the house, though they had been only feet apart, Jacob had still felt as though he were being addressed from afar, amidst a crowd like the one in which he was now entangled.

"We have come together to renew our bonds of community, to strengthen our chosen path to Truesight," the voice resonated

The crowd responded to the familiar prompt, chanting in unison, "Blindness is purity. Blindness is unity. Blindness is freedom."

Jacob recited the Foundation's motto with the others, but his words were mumbled, his voice low.

The councilor spoke again from the platform at the far end of the square. "For today's Gathering, the East Tier chorus will perform a song recently composed by the musicians of our sister colony on Pollard. It is extraordinary."

A moment of silence elapsed. Then the group on the platform began to sing. The small chorus, five women and five men, sounded much larger, their voices magnified by the speakers in the square. As the music washed over them, the crowd gasped at its beauty. Even Jacob's mother, who was often critical of others' performances, drew in her breath and squeezed his hand as the music surrounded them. Words were sung, but Jacob wasn't listening to them. They were just beautiful sounds that absorbed his earlier unease and carried it away. Though the rhythm and dynamics varied, the song's tempo was quick and light, an intricate dance of notes. There was no instrumental accompaniment; none was needed. Instead the voices themselves seemed to assume the timbre of strings and horns.

The song ended and Harmony exploded in applause. Jacob joined in. He felt whole again, connected to the mass of people expressing their appreciation to the chorus. The feeling of peace lingered, leaving him dazed and barely listening to the high councilor's speech to the community. It didn't matter, though. The brief sermon was usually a variation on a single theme—Harmony Station and the Foundation represented the pinnacle of human virtue and self-fulfillment, a model for the rest of humanity. Occasionally a diatribe would be vented against the Seers, a reference to a recent tragedy somewhere among the settled worlds. The speech usually concluded with a list of Harmony's recent accomplishments—which team of growers had gathered the highest yield that week, a sculptor who had created a new fountain in the South Tier square, a particular student who had been chosen to visit Earth for advanced study with the Foundation. On occasion, before everyone left, there were announcements.

Sometimes these took the form of chastisements, such as a warning to conserve food or water or a reminder about a rule. Today an announcement was made, and Jacob tuned back in as the high councilor concluded.

"Citizens of Harmony: tomorrow evening there will be a delivery. Growers will remain in the fields at their stations as usual. All others will observe the curfew and remain at home after the dinner hour. This delivery is important. I've arranged for Harmony to receive a shipment of food supplies to supplement our own stores until the harvest. That is all."

The four horns sounded at each corner of the square, their different pitches guiding citizens in the proper direction toward home. The crowd began to dissemble, sorting themselves toward various exits, quietly seeping out of the square like an evaporating mist. Once back on the avenues, sounders rang once again, growing quieter as people separated into smaller groups along the side streets. Jacob walked with his mother, listening to the excited voices talking about tomorrow's delivery and its promise of better meals. People always became excited when there was a delivery, no matter what its contents. Once they were home, he asked his mother the reason why.

"I don't know. Something different, I suppose. A break from routine."

"Have you ever been to one?" he asked.

"Of course not. Everyone's at home during a curfew," she reminded him. "Who cares, anyway? I'm sure it's quite boring. The Seers come in with their haulers, drop off a bunch of crates, and go home. That's it." She sounded impatient, as though she was waiting for something.

"Then, why do we have to stay indoors?"

"For our own protection, probably. It's unsafe to have people on the street with a bunch of vehicles, men, and boxes moving in every direction."

Suddenly realizing his father hadn't joined them after the Gathering, Jacob asked, "Where's Dad?"

"He'll be home soon." It occurred to Jacob that maybe she didn't know. "In the meantime I'm tired. You should go to bed too. You have to deliver your report tomorrow, don't you?"

That's right, he did. He had nearly forgotten about it. Fortunately he'd finished it a week ago. He had practiced with his mother and his father at different times until it was firmly committed to memory. Tomorrow he would repeat the same words, only in front of the class. Since he was scheduled last, he had already heard everyone else's speeches and knew he could do as good a job. He would simply stand in front and press the play button in his memory, like the lesson players in the library. No, he wasn't worried about the report; it was something else that kept him from leaving the room.

"Ma, I haven't been feeling good the last few days. I keep getting headaches."

"So what? My head aches all the time. Take one of my pills if you want." She sounded like his father all of a sudden.

"I was going to, but the headaches don't stay long enough to bother; they go as quickly as they come."

"Come here," she said. She put her cheek against his forehead. "You don't feel feverish. I'm sure you're fine. Just growing pains, that's all. If you're still having them next week, I'll try to arrange a visit to the infirmary. Wait a minute"—she stopped him as he turned to go—"this is about tomorrow, isn't it? You're trying to weasel out of giving your report."

"No, I'm not," he said. He knew she was teasing him, but it irritated him anyway. He went to his room, got ready for bed, and crawled under the covers. He heard his father come home just as he was falling asleep. He drifted off to the sound of his parents' subdued, angry voices muffled through the door.

# CHAPTER FIVE

"Okay, Jacob. Time for your report," Mrs. Lawson prompted. Jacob stood before the class, swaying slightly in the midday sun. As they did on occasion, the students were sitting on the lawn behind the school, a level plane of grass thirty yards square. "Some fresh air today," the teacher had said.

"We've saved Jacob's report for last because, in many ways, his is the most important," Mrs. Lawson continued. "We will end our presentations by going back to the beginning. Jacob will speak on the origins of the Foundation."

The obligatory applause sounded from the class, and Jacob prepared to speak. He found it difficult to concentrate. A haze had been crowding into his brain all morning, gathering like a heavy storm, punctuated by distant lightning flares of pain. Upon standing, the aching intensified, concentrating in his brow. He was sure that insects were crawling along his face, stinging at the edges of his eyes. He closed them and the burning subsided noticeably, dwindling to almost nothing. With reluctance, he opened them. Again, the pain resurfaced, but not as intensely. In its place a brightness so faint it was merely a gray glow hung before him. He blinked several times. He didn't know what brightness was; he only knew that when he closed his eyes, that which was before him changed, and changed again when he raised his lids.

"Jacob, let's go. We're waiting," Mrs. Lawson stated impatiently.

*I can do this*, Jacob told himself. He pushed aside the bizarre sensation flooding his consciousness, let go the words he had heard and spoken so many times.

"The Foundation was created in 2102 by Francis and Jean Aldrich from the city of Toronto in a nation known as Canada. Prior to its creation, many parents had been selecting the characteristics of their children for several decades—everything from gender to eye and hair color—through genetic engineering. Both Francis and Jean had been born blind. They wanted their children to be a part of their way of life, so they decided that their children would share this trait, creating the first generation of children intentionally born with what some considered a disability. The publicity generated by the event persuaded several other couples in Canada and the United States to do the same."

Now the dim gray glow grew to ash, trembled and surged, flirted with silver before finally receding to black. Again the wave passed through him as he stood paralyzed. A voice, sounding small and distant, asked what was happening. He realized it was his own voice, the voice inside his head asking a question for which he had no answer. He realized he had stopped speaking, that everyone waited. How long had he been standing in silence?

Jacob cleared his throat and continued, his voice weaker. "Many people criticized the Aldriches and other parents for the choice they made. They argued that these parents were saddling their children with a burden, that they were doing no less than inflicting cruelty on them. Other, good people, however, hailed the Aldriches for their brave decision. They denounced the critics for their bigotry, for attempting to impose their own cultural prejudices. Heartened by their supporters and aided by an endowment from the Robertson Corporation—an aeronautics company whose founder, Lowell Robertson, was himself blind—the Aldriches and several other sightless families purchased a thousand acres of land and organized the first community on the continent of Australia. Soon blind people from all over Earth began to settle in the community, now named Robertson. Inspired by Eastern spiritualism and a seventeenth-century group called the Puritans, Francis, Jean, and their friends formulated the philosophy they called Truesight."

Jacob stopped. A new wave was approaching; he could feel it. He braced himself as it flared brighter and brighter, this time not fading to black, but holding steady. The light, incredible in the midday sun, penetrated his being. It shone around him as he turned his head—brighter in some places, darker in others, but ever present. Even when he closed his eyes, a part of the brightness remained, though it was a different shade when filtered through the membrane of his eyelids. He opened his eyes again. Now the light was fragmented, brighter above, darker below. In the darker area lighter patches, round in shape, floated before him. He felt dizzy.

"Go on, Jacob, you're doing a fine job," Mrs. Lawson encouraged.

Jacob took several deep breaths and closed his eyes again. Still the light burned before him. "I don't feel good," he murmured. A couple of students giggled. He brought both hands up and covered his eyes, pressing hard against his face to smother the fire. It worked; the brightness was gone. He kept his hands in place. As long as he didn't remove them, everything would be all right, the way it was before.

"You're only nervous, Jacob. Now please, finish your report, and afterward I'll send you to the infirmary."

The darkness of the cool hands calmed him. He continued. "By the time Francis Aldrich died, at the turn of the century, the Foundation was firmly established and Robertson had grown to a sizable and thriving community, branching out to form a sister community in New Zealand named after Aldrich. Truesight became a more widely respected philosophy. Some even voluntarily became blind through surgery and moved to Robertson. These people were called Oedipi, named after the ancient hero Oedipus who, in rejecting the evil of the world, bravely chose the path of blindness. To this day Oedipi, like Egan's father"—as he had planned earlier, Jacob paused here to honor his friend—"continue to be among the most respected members of the Foundation, having overcome the limitations of their former sight."

The words now flowed quickly. More than anything, he wanted to be done. He felt self-conscious standing before everyone, hands covering his face; no one knew what he was doing, what lay beneath his hands. Still, it felt like a deceit, though he didn't quite know what he was hiding.

Drops of sweat were forming on his forehead, trickling down behind his ear and onto his neck as he pressed on. "Things were not perfect, however. Over the course of several generations, the Foundation remained the victim of criticism and occasional physical assault. The August Day Massacre—in which four Foundation members were killed and a dozen wounded on August fifth, 2193, by a group of antigenetic terrorists—led the Western Compact to grant the Foundation protected status, which it retains to this day, both on Earth and among the settled worlds. In the centuries since then, the Foundation has spread throughout explored space, free from harassment, and has striven to become a model to humanity. The end."

The abrupt conclusion surprised the class, the teacher, and himself. Finally a smattering of applause sounded from the students. Mrs. Lawson cleared her throat. "You ended a little quickly, Jacob. Did you want to say more?" she asked.

He did have more material, but he just couldn't go on. "No, I'm done," he answered weakly. He sat down and uncovered his face. The brightness remained. When he opened his eyes, he felt a little dizzier. He just wanted to go home.

"Well," she said, "unfortunately, your grade will

suffer for ending so abruptly, but what you did say was excellent. You certainly know the history."

Did he? he wondered. As if inflamed by the stinging light, he grew annoyed at the patronizing tone of the teacher's last remark. He had said what he was supposed to say, but the more he thought about it, the less he was sure what much of it meant. What was "Eastern philosophy" or "aeronautics"? Who were the Puritans? He didn't know much about Oedipus, beyond his brief remark. A pulsating tone sounded in the background, the sound of a finder. The students began to whisper to one another, wondering who was carrying the rare device. The sound grew louder and faster as it approached, then stopped. A male voice unfamiliar to Jacob called for the teacher, who left the group and went off to the side for a hushed discussion.

Jacob could sense the other children around him creep forward slowly, quietly, in the direction of the voices. They were eager to find out about the surprise visit and had forgotten about him. He didn't join them. He sat and blinked his eyes. Off and on, off and on, the light before him flashed. Undistracted by having to perform before the class, he turned his head slowly as the sensation of light altered, shifting with the movement of his head from up to down and side to side. It suddenly occurred to him, deep inside, so slightly he could hardly grasp it, what could be happening to him. What shouldn't be happening to him. He knew but was unable to say it, unable to admit it to himself. But he knew.

The voice disappeared, the finder slowly beeping after a new target, and Mrs. Lawson addressed the class. "I have just been told that the delivery will occur earlier than scheduled. Therefore your afternoon session is canceled. Everyone in Harmony is to report home immediately. Curfew will commence in one hour." She dismissed the students and everyone parted for home. Though no one said a word around Mrs. Lawson, Jacob could sense their elation. He wondered why this dismissal couldn't have happened ten minutes ago and saved him the embarrassment of curtailing his report. Still, the idea of going home was preferable to sitting through an afternoon of class. Everything that had happened, that was happening right now, overwhelmed and exhausted him, leaving him empty and confused. He was so distracted he barely heard the familiar pitch of Egan's sounder approaching from behind.

"Hey," Egan whispered in his ear, coming up beside him and taking his arm once they were well away from school, "I have an idea." Jacob groaned—he knew what was coming. "Let's check out the delivery."

"And how are we going to do that?" Jacob asked. "Our parents will never let us out during a curfew."

"Come on, it'll be easy for you. Your father's out in the fields, so it's only your mother. You just said you felt sick. Tell her you're not feeling good and that you want to go to bed, and then sneak out. Listen, you bailed out on me the last time I asked you to have some fun. I'm starting to wonder about you."

"What about you?" Jacob shot back.

"Don't worry about me; I have my own techniques of escape," Egan assured him.

Jacob hesitated. Maybe he should go. Maybe the adventure would serve as a distraction. Besides, he had refused Egan last week about borrowing the finder; he didn't want to seem too much like a coward. "All right. But how do we avoid getting caught?"

"Okay, I've thought about that. All we do is leave our sounders at home. We'll be totally silent and the listeners won't be able to track us."

"What about the delivery workers? They are Seers, you know."

"True, but the curfew always starts well before they arrive—I heard my father say so once. We simply leave right after it starts and find a hiding place. You know that little rise just above the drop-off point near the storehouses? We'll slip over there and hide in the tall grass. They'll never be able to see us; I'm sure of it."

It was a good plan, Jacob had to agree. Still, it sounded almost too easy, but he couldn't tell Egan that. Egan depended on enthusiasm, and Jacob had always responded in kind. Now, however, his friend's energy and certainty made Jacob more conscious of his own uncertainties, more aware of his own confusion and pain.

"Jake?" Egan shook him. "Are you there? I'm talking to you!"

"Sorry," Jacob said, "I was thinking."

"Of course. Jacob the thinker. Don't think too much, okay? That's what my father says. And you know what—he's right."

"I suppose," Jacob agreed. Nevertheless, the plan sounded too easy.

"When curfew starts, wait ten minutes and then meet me behind the school," Egan said, turning onto his street. "We'll go together from there, and remember to forget your sounder."

Egan took off. Jacob listened to him go, until he disappeared around the bend, before continuing home. He wondered how his friend could break the rules so easily. After all, his father was an Oedipi, sent directly by the Foundation to assist the council. He was an important person. Maybe that's why Egan acted that way—he probably figured he could get away with it, even if he was caught. Would that bubble of safety cover Jacob as well? Probably not. His father wasn't important; he was a grower. His job was important, but he wasn't. His mother was more prominent, but still, several musicians in Harmony were as skilled as she was.

Jacob picked up the pace, walking with abandon, not caring if he ran into anything or anyone. He was angry with himself for thinking those thoughts about his parents, angry with Egan for being both carefree and powerful, and angry at all the circumstances in his life that he couldn't control. He shut his eyes and this time kept them closed, slipped back into the darkness all the way home. Only when he'd shut the door behind him did he dare to open them again, and all remained dark in the underground house.

His mother was there, practicing a new composition on the antique piano. She barely noticed when Jacob told her he wasn't feeling good and was going to bed. He went to his room and shut the door most of the way, being careful not to latch it. He pulled his sounder off his shirt and tossed it on the bureau, where it landed with a metallic thud before clinking off the music box. Flopping onto the bed, he lay back and listened to the notes drifting from the living room, hanging in the dark.

The music stopped when his mother went into the kitchen. Then, distant but loud enough to be heard through the earthen walls of his home, a siren wailed. Curfew had begun.

# CHAPTER SIX

*Why am I here?* Jacob thought as he leaned against the back wall of the schoolhouse. *Because it's Egan*, he realized. In another few weeks school would be over. Then they would be busy working in the fields, helping with the harvest for those two weeks of service, like most members of the community. After that, who knew? Whatever the specialization assigned to him, he knew that it would be different from Egan's. Once they began their training, they wouldn't be spending much time together. So here he was, for what would probably be one last adventure, as Egan referred to them. To this point it had been fairly easy. His mother had resumed playing by the time he left, hammering out notes that filled every room of the house, and was so focused on her music she wouldn't have noticed if Jacob had slammed the door on his way out. After that, slipping along the empty streets was simple.

Surveying the brightness around him, he had a difficult time feeling that anything else mattered right now. Even his recent fears for Delaney diminished in the strange glow that engulfed him. When he left the house, the light had relented from earlier in the day and the air had cooled, as if the sun had decided not to burn so hotly. A pressure filled the air now, a heaviness that reminded him of the Gathering last night. He could sense a storm was coming. Again and again he blinked, amazed and frightened at the novelty of the experience. By now the pain had vanished, but the realization of what was happening to him offered its own pain. For the first time he admitted it to himself. He was seeing, or at least starting to. But this unnavigable blur of light and shadows couldn't actually be sight, could it? He suspected he was on his way, however, and could only wonder how far he would go. Until now, he could hold on to a glimmer of doubt that he was beginning to see. He could hope that this changing awareness was not the thing his entire world was structured against. He could hope that it would disappear, along with the memory, and he would be left behind to continue as he was—a boy dealing with the normal fears of a normal life.

But as Jacob had walked through the town on his way to the school, he had known that it was real. He could see the lighter strip above—which he assumed was the sky—stretching all the way across his awareness, slipping down into the middle, where the street ran straight before him. As before, he noticed the darker patch below the horizon, the earth rising up to either side, where he knew the hills and houses lay. He wondered if he should tell Egan about what was happening to him. Or reveal it to anyone. The thought made him queasy. How could he possibly tell anyone he was becoming a Seer? Still, the idea of keeping this terrible secret hidden—pretending everything was normal, everything was fine—seemed much worse. It went against everything he had been taught—that there were no secrets in Harmony.

Where was Egan, anyway? Jacob had been early and lived closer to the school, but Egan should have arrived about five minutes ago. *He better not be bailing out on me*, Jacob thought. No, if Egan hadn't arrived yet, there was a good reason. Maybe his father was being more vigilant than usual. Jacob had known Mr. Spencer for several years and had decided that he was the most suspicious person he had ever met. Perhaps part of it had to do with having a son like Egan, who would give anyone a reason to be suspicious. Still, Egan's father sometimes gave Jacob an uneasy, almost guilty feeling. The man was continually asking him questions whenever he went to visit Egan, wanting to know about Jacob's neighbors, about his teachers— what did they do? Had they ever mentioned this matter or that idea? Jacob didn't like it and felt sorry for Egan, though he probably shouldn't, since Egan himself didn't seem to take his father too seriously.

He waited a few more minutes and then left. Egan would know where to find him; it was his plan, after all. Moving away from the schoolhouse, Jacob walked as quickly as he could, crossing to the more isolated back streets, and then followed the path that led to the store-houses. He began hearing voices. At first he froze instinctively, as if waiting for the inevitable approach and apprehension. He realized, however, that the voices he heard were far away. He relaxed and continued until the storehouses loomed as dark shapes against the brightness of the sky. Though still distant, the voices were closer now and to his left, coming from the other side of the buildings. He hurried to the back of the nearest structure, around the corner from where the workers waited for the arrival of the Seers. He could hear the high councilor's voice among them, issuing orders.

In the distance came a deep rumbling sound, a bass that he seemed to feel as much as hear. Steadily it grew. It must be the haulers. Under cover of the noise they provided, he slipped away from the buildings and in the direction of the hill behind the cluster of storehouses, entering the tall grass. He dropped to his hands and knees and began crawling up the bank; the tall blades of coarse grass scratched his face and hands as he pushed them aside. By now the rumble of the haulers was incredible. They sounded as if they were about to come rolling down right on top of him. For a moment he panicked, wondering if he had put himself directly in their path. But he knew that thought was ridiculous; they were coming from the other side of the buildings, and he was safe. He stopped to listen, hearing them pull closer before coming to a stop. Their engines wound down and the rushing hiss of hydraulics announced their arrival.

Feeling exposed on the hillside, he picked his way through the cover until he could sense that he had gone up and over the rise. He rolled down the back side of the hill a few yards and came to rest in the grass. He stayed motionless for a moment and caught his breath, looking into the sky that was a gray blur, the tall grass a fuzzy dimness at the edges. *Where is Egan?* he wondered again. He couldn't sense anyone nearby, but that meant nothing. He listened to the commotion of the delivery on the other side of the hill so he could tell his friend later, but heard little. A few indistinguishable voices shouted commands back and forth. He also heard the lowing of cattle. They must be the new stock his father had mentioned earlier. The wind, which had started to pick up in the last ten minutes, began to intensify, rustling the grass, making it difficult to hear above the swishing.

He decided to seek a better vantage point and scuttled back toward the crest and along the top. He heard the sudden rustle at his feet but it was too late. Something heavy fell across his shins and instantly he was tumbling through the air and into the grass, letting out a muffled grunt. He had tripped over someone's leg and was scrambling to rise when a foot drove into his back, a blind kick that knocked him down again. He turned over and lunged back toward the assailant, tackling the figure and pinning its arms against the ground.

"Stop it, Egan! It's only me," he hissed.

"Jacob?" a girl's voice cried out in surprise.

"Delaney?" he gasped, equally in shock. He rolled off her and sat in the grass, panting as adrenaline flooded his body.

"What are you doing here?" she demanded, moving away.

"I was meeting Egan here to check out the delivery." He winced, wishing he hadn't mentioned his friend, though he knew she wouldn't tell. "What about you? What are you doing here?" She didn't answer. Suddenly he understood. "You're going to try to leave again, aren't you? You're going to run away."

"I have to go, Jacob. I have to do it this way; I don't have any choice."

"This is crazy. How are you going to get out of here, anyway? They can see you, you know. Maybe not us, but those other men can. Are you just going to walk down there, in front of everyone, and hop in the back of a hauler, no questions asked? You're only going to get in trouble again."

"I have to try it. I have to do something," she whispered.

"Laney," he pleaded, "this is wrong. What makes you think leaving will make everything better?"

"Great. First my father and now you, too?" Her voice simmered with contempt, but he persisted.

"How are they going to react to this? My mother, your father? How is this going to affect *everyone*?"

"Don't think I haven't considered that. I have, over and over. But even more, I think about what's out there, what it must be like in a different place. Sometimes it's all I can think about, and then I feel I can never be happy here."

Jacob couldn't speak. The whole conversation was too strange to really be happening. He sat there, feeling powerless, feeling the wind against his face, listening to the bang of crates, the calling of men, and the lowing of cattle below.

"I sound desperate, don't I?" She tried to laugh. It came out sounding hollow and forced. "Well, I am. I'm just sad. A sad case."

"If you try to leave, I'll yell. Right now I'll yell and they'll come. I swear I will," he whispered.

"No, you won't. We're friends, aren't we, Jake?" She reached out and brushed his shoulder, held his hand.

Yes, he thought, of course they were. But what was a friend supposed to do in this situation, a situation that was never supposed to happen in the first place? He wasn't sure. What would the rules say? The rules would say he should report her immediately. But the rules also said he should never be here to begin with. When he didn't answer, she spoke again, raising her voice against a gust of wind.

"Jacob, I don't expect you to understand. Just trust me when I say it's too late for me. If I don't get away with this delivery, it's over. My father—"

"We can hear you there!" a voice called from the hillside a dozen yards away. "Stop, both of you, and stand up!" a man ordered, his voice growing louder as he crested the ridge.

"Run!" Delaney screamed.

Without thinking, Jacob raced in the opposite direction of the voice. The wind roared. The only other sound was the beating of blood in his ears and the gasping of his breath as he tore through the grass. He stopped momentarily to listen and catch his breath, panic rising in his chest. Where was Delaney? Where was he? He had to think. He had to listen. He had to be smart and get his bearings. A listener must have heard them and cried out—the Seers wouldn't have been able to see them behind the hilltop, or even care if they had, would they? He thought he could hear shouting in the distance, but the voices didn't sound close. He figured the listeners either weren't chasing him or were moving in the wrong direction. If they used a Seer to help them, he was finished. He could only hope that they wanted to avoid the embarrassment and not call on them, or that the Seers would be too indifferent to interfere.

Bounding through the grass, Jacob rushed in the direction he thought would return him to his home, back to some street where he could at least stop and get his bearings. The ground was level, which made his going easier, but he stumbled several times, distracted by fear and the echo of Delaney's haunted voice. He paused for a moment and wondered what had happened to her. Had she been caught? Did she escape after all? He began running again, this time frantically, lifting his feet high to avoid the tangling grass. The wind changed directions and began blowing in his face. For the first time, he realized he was crying, the breeze accentuating the tears streaked cool across his cheeks. He ran for what seemed like forever, trapped in a dream, in that nightmare where no matter how fast or far he tried to go, he went nowhere.

With a thud, Jacob tripped and fell. The blades of grass scratched him, their fibers biting into his skin. Burying his face in his arms, he began to cry openly and just gave in to it, listening to the long sobs as though it were someone else who was weeping, somebody else's pain that he had nothing to do with. Swallowed by the grass, the wind blowing stronger, blocking the possibility of any other sound, he felt alone, as if he were the only person who existed, as if all life had disappeared beyond this sphere of grass within the plains. He felt so tired. Maybe he could just stay here and rest, sleep in this cocoon and awake to find himself someone else, someone still blind, someone who wasn't confused and powerless, who didn't know that other people struggled unhappily with their reality.

He was ready to drift off when something soft brushed against his face, startling him. He froze in the grass, not certain what to do. Suddenly a gentle purring murmured in his ear, and a scratchy tongue licked at the dampness along the contour of his face. He sighed with relief and brought the cat toward him. It was a big cat, heavy, with a sleek coat that rolled in his hands as he pulled the animal to him. He lay back with the cat upon his chest, scratching its ears and back, listening to it purr. After a minute it tensed to leave, but Jacob held on. It struggled against his hands until, sick of the game, it turned and swatted a paw against his face. He winced as the tips of its claws caught his nose, and he let go. The cat disappeared, silent and back on the hunt.

He wiped the tears from his face. The crying had run its course and the universe had returned. Picking himself up again, Jacob continued forward, slower now, trying to estimate the distance toward the settlement. The blur of light and dark between land and sky was no help at all, and the difference was less pronounced as the sky darkened with clouds. Time and space seemed distorted as he worked the riddle of movement in his mind. It seemed like he had traveled too far, that he should have found some path a while ago. On the other hand, it also felt as if he had been running for hours, when it couldn't have been more than ten or fifteen minutes since Delaney screamed for him to escape. After a minute he felt his right hand brush against a pathminder. A step later the gravel crunched beneath his feet, and he could feel the repellent strength of the beam, its semicircle of force focused on the street side only. Not sure which way to go, he chose right, hoping to find some familiar landmark that could lead him home. All he desired now was his own room and his own bed, where he could sleep and forget this entire day.

He finally had a bit of luck. After walking only a few dozen yards, he could hear the North Tier fountain in the distance, one of the many fountains scattered throughout the settlement, each with its own distinctive collection of waterfalls and spraying patterns; this one was Jacob's favorite. It was made of smooth rock, saved from the initial clearing of Harmony's fields. It was also the tallest, with a built-in slide on one side, which Jacob and his friends, as young children, used to slip down on hot summer days. Best of all, it was located in his own section of Harmony, only a three-minute walk down a few streets to home.

He quickened his pace and entered the small square dominated by the fountain. He approached its edge and dipped his hands in, scooping a handful of water to his mouth. It tasted treated, more so than most of the water in Harmony, but it was cool. He drank, scooping several more times, cupping both hands together. He hadn't realized he was so thirsty. The staccato clip of the three spigots spraying in unison from the top of the fountain rained a gentle mist on him. He leaned in and felt the cool spray coating his face. He blinked as the water stung his open eyes and, stepping back, glanced at the sky, dimmer now but bright enough to silhouette the dark fountain rising above him. Splashing more water on his face, he felt the sting of tiny cuts and scratches on his face and arms. He quickly washed himself to remove the film of tears and sweat, gasping at the coldness. He wanted to linger and listen to the clicking jets of water, ticking like his mother's metronome against the rush of tiny waterfalls and gurgling rivulets that cascaded down all sides of the fountain and into its collecting pool, but he had to go. He was already unbelievably lucky to have made it this far; the listeners would certainly scan the entire colony after the incident on the ridge.

He traced his way down the last turn and arrived home. No sound emanated from the street; everyone was subdued by the curfew. He listened at his door, hoping for the sound of his mother's piano that would give him the chance to sneak in undetected, but silence greeted him. He turned the latch gently, making sure there was no click of metal against metal that sounded when he normally opened the door. With even speed and pressure he swung the door open quickly, in a way that avoided the usual squeaks. He listened again. All was quiet. *She must be sleeping*, he thought with relief, closed the door behind him, and made for his room through the dark.

"Jacob, stop." He froze at the sound of his mother's voice. For a moment he thought desperately for an excuse, some lie to prove he had never left, but he figured it would only make matters worse. She would already have checked his room and realized he had left and was returning. "You forgot this," she said. A small metal object bounced off his chest and rattled to the floor. It was his sounder. "Well?"

"Well, what? There's nothing to say," he replied, and immediately cringed at his response. He needed to be conciliatory, make a show of remorse. And it wouldn't be fake—he really was sorry he had ever left to begin with. And now this, the perfect end to a horrible day. No. It could be worse. He could really have been caught. He could be sitting right now with the listeners in detention.

"There's a lot to say, Jake. You idiot!" Jacob felt as though he had been struck. She had never called him names, saving nasty words for his father. She was furious. "I cannot believe you would violate curfew. It's just something that—people don't do it, that's all."

"I'm sorry, Ma. I know. It was stupid."

"Okay, then. Good, Jacob. Everything's suddenly fixed. No problem."

He hated her sarcasm. What did she want him to say? This was almost as bad as the conversation with Delaney. Thinking about Delaney suddenly helped him, made him feel better in a way. It put this whole ugly scene into perspective. What did this matter? Not at all. His mother's anger, which was probably equally mixed with fear, would disappear by tomorrow. It always had in the past.

"Can I go to bed?" he asked, his voice as neutral as possible.

"We're not finished. First you get a warning for not activating your sounder, and now this. I don't want to know what the punishment for this would be. I could be demoted, or your father. You could ruin any chance for a decent specialization. You want to be stuck out in the fields, working with your father?" She sounded so contemptuous.

"Why do you always have to go after him?" he retorted. "You're talking about me right now. Remember?" What did she know about the future? What could she understand about his problems, about what he was dealing with?

"You want to go to bed?" She was holding back tears. "Fine, go to bed. When Richard gets home, I'm going to tell him about this, and tomorrow we're all going to have a talk. Now go away and leave me alone!"

She was practically screaming. He marched quickly to his room and slammed the door.

For a few moments he stood there, his chest heaving. He wanted to punch the door, kick the bed, do *something*. Without thinking, he groped across the bureau top, grabbed his music box, and threw it against the wall. He could hear it smash in the darkness, raining fragments of metal that tinkled as they scattered across the floor. Collapsing onto the bed, he drew the pillow over his face. A moment later he could hear the piano notes sailing down the hall and into his room. His mother was back at it. This time she played furiously, pounding the keys, sending minor chords flying around the house, beating against his door. He listened to her play an entire song, and then another, and another, each song equally intense. Jacob pressed the pillow against his ears, but the sound still penetrated. He couldn't escape its terror or its beauty.

Removing the pillow from his ears, Jacob sat up in bed and listened. She had stopped playing midsong. Getting up from his bed, he crept to the door and opened it a crack. He could hear voices in the foyer—his mother's and a man's. At first he thought his father had returned, and his heartbeat quickened, imagining the conversation that was occurring. He moved silently into the hallway and discovered the man's voice wasn't his father's, but a stranger's. His blood pounded harder now at the realization, and he edged himself closer until he could make out the words.

"You say you never left this evening?"

"That's what I said. I've been practicing all evening. I have an important recital next month, and it's occupied all my time."

"We know your husband is on duty right now. What about your son, Jacob?"

"My son has been with me all night. He wasn't feeling well and went to bed early."

"What's wrong with him?"

Jacob's heart beat louder now. He covered his chest, as if he could muffle the sound he was certain they must be able to hear.

"I don't know. He didn't say. He went straight to bed."

"Maybe you should have him examined by the healer," the man offered.

"Maybe I will," she responded, her voice even and controlled. Jacob marveled at her composure.

The man, probably a listener, continued barraging her with questions. "You were playing unusually loud when I came to the door. Aren't you concerned that the noise might wake him?"

"Jacob's a heavy sleeper. Besides, he's used to my

playing." A pause ensued, as if the visitation were a game and they were both trying to determine their next move. She spoke next. "Why did you say you were here again?"

He didn't answer but began moving toward the hallway. "Your son's room is down here?" Most homes in Harmony had the same layout.

"Yes, at the end," she said quietly.

The man paused about ten feet from Jacob. Jacob leaned flat against the wall, frozen in terror.

"Do you mind if I check on him?" he asked. Without waiting for a reply, he continued. Jacob held his breath, feeling the air around him stir as the man passed within a foot of him. In a panic Jacob realized his door was open. The listener was nearly at the bedroom doorway when a knock sounded at the front door. Jacob heard the man stop and turn.

"Shall I get it?" his mother asked.

"That's okay, I will," the man said. He breezed by Jacob as he returned to the foyer and opened the door. Another man, who Jacob guessed was also a listener, called to his partner, and the two had a brief, subdued discussion on the doorstep. Then they disappeared, without another word to Jacob's mother, who quickly closed the door. She didn't move for several moments, and he could hear her breathing with heavy, quick gasps. The calm facade had faded, replaced by a struggle to regain her composure. Jacob returned to his bedroom, quietly closing the door. Part of him wanted to rush out, hug her, and thank her for saving him; after their earlier scene, however, he thought she might not appreciate his thanks, since he was responsible for the encounter.

Instead he removed his clothes and climbed into bed. He thought about what she had just done. She had lied for him. She had broken one of the cardinal rules of the community and lied—to a listener, no less. From the first day of school, Jacob had been taught that in Harmony everyone's first duty was to the community. Truth was the most important virtue, as Delaney's father had stated many times at the Gatherings. He wasn't disappointed in his mother—it would be foolish to feel that way, given the circumstances—but part of him was surprised. She had lied to save him. She had lied to save herself, too, he realized. He wondered which was more important to her. *No, that's unfair,* he thought. She could have reported him. Maybe she would have been rewarded. What bothered him most, though, was how they knew to come here, to his house. Had Delaney been caught? Had she told on him? Maybe they had recognized his voice. Maybe he hadn't been alone at all; they could have followed him home. Maybe they would come again tomorrow, this time for him.

As he lay in bed, his mother resumed her practice. This time the tempo was slow, melancholy, and the notes, sustained by the ancient floor pedal, hovered in the air. He could also hear the wind wheezing through the tiny air vent that led from his room to the outside. He knew that only the strongest gusts could cause the high-pitched whine that rose and fell from the narrow grate near the ceiling, as if crying in accompaniment to the classical étude his mother played on the antique piano.

He fell into a fitful sleep, turning restlessly, until several hours later when he heard his mother's voice calling him, rousing him from slumber. He could tell by her raspy voice that she had been crying, that something was terribly wrong. As he sat up in bed she embraced and held him.

"What's the matter?" he asked, not really wanting her to answer.

"Jake," she whispered in a hoarse voice, "it's Delaney," she said, and began to sob. "She's dead."

# CHAPTER SEVEN

"How can that be?" Jacob cried. Delaney couldn't be dead. He had just seen her hours ago, had spoken to her, had touched her. He began to feel sick, as if he was going to throw up. "How do you know?" he asked. "Who told you?"

"Jim Mason just came over from across the street. The news is traveling all over Harmony. He said that Martin found her, but that's all I know." She began to cry again. It took Jacob a moment to remember that Delaney's father was named Martin. He jumped from the bed and, after groping for his clothes, began shakily to dress.

"What are you doing?" his mother asked.

"I have to get Dad," he said, his voice also shaky.

"No, Jacob. His shift is almost over—he'll be home in less than an hour. Besides, Jim said that a storm is moving in. Your father is probably on his way home already."

"He should be here. He needs to be here." Jacob didn't really know what he was saying. He just needed to get out of this room, this house. He had to do something.

"Jacob, don't go. You've already been out once today. Don't go again. I need you here," she cried.

"I can't stay. I'll be back soon," he said, and left, slamming the door behind him.

As soon as he entered the street, a gust struck him full on, thrusting him backward for a moment. It was night and the sky was dark. He could see nothing, but he could hear the rumble of thunder in the distance, far deeper than the noise the haulers had made earlier that evening. Occasionally a brief flash altered his awareness. He remembered learning about the electrical discharges that caused thunder. His teacher had called it lightning and now he knew why. He pushed ahead, the wind roaring in his ears, pushing back tears that he realized were streaming from his eyes. *Twice in one day*, he thought. He hadn't cried in more than two years, had prided himself on that, and here he was, hours later, weeping again. He didn't care, though. Delaney was dead.

*No, she's not*, he told himself. It was too terrible to be true. *She's not, she's not.* He kept saying it as he ran, began yelling it into the indifferent storm, its wind throwing the words right back in his face. He passed to the outskirts of town, moving as quickly as he could against the wind. Rain was beginning to fall. The thick drops splattered on his face, stinging him and running down his cheeks, mingling with the tears. The thunder was louder now as the storm swept across the plains. The lightning flashes grew brighter and more frequent. By the time he reached the edge of town and had started down the wide lane that led to the fields, he was running with abandon. The brief flashes illuminated the blurry straightness cutting through the dark. He fell more than once on the road, which was slippery with mud. Each time he picked himself up and wiped the mud from his face. He didn't care that he was dirty or wet, or that he was crying, or that his elbow was now throbbing from having hit a rock on the path during the last fall. He didn't even care if he found his father. All he wanted to do was run, to lose himself in the storm, in the wind that seemed to strip away all conscious thought. He wanted to forget the words, the voice that had continued to creep along the edges of his mind from the first moment his mother told him Delaney was dead.

*It's your fault*, the voice said again. He had been with her. He had talked to her. If he had spoken the right words, this would never have happened. He should have told his mother about the encounter earlier so she could have done something. Or maybe he should have helped Delaney escape; then she would be far away and alive, on her way to what she wanted. He could even have escaped with her, protected her. All these thoughts flew around in his head. He kept throwing them away, but they kept returning as he ran, clutching his elbow. The lightning was flashing all around him now, the thunderclaps piling up and hammering him from all sides. A dark shape appeared before him from nowhere, highlighted by a series of flashes, and he suddenly found himself prostrate, gasping from the collision.

"What the hell?" a man cried out. "Something just hit me!"

"It was me," Jacob hollered, trying to be heard above the wind and thunder. He suddenly felt two strong hands reach out, find his arms, and pull him to his feet. A wet hand moved along his face.

"What's going on here?" another man shouted, joining them.

"It's a kid. I think. He just ran into me," the first man explained.

"Who are you?" the second man yelled.

"Jacob," Jacob screamed. "Jacob Manford."

"Richard's boy?" the first man asked. "Hey,

Richard!" the man shouted through the storm. "Get over here! It's your son!"

Lightning pulsed an irregular heartbeat of illumination. Under its flare Jacob could see a bright shape emerge from the storm and approach him. "Jacob?" his father cried. "What are you doing here? We have to get home. The storm rolled in quicker than we thought."

Jacob grabbed him by both arms and leaned his forehead against his father's chest. "Delaney's dead!" he shouted to his father. The thunder was booming, crashing in waves that seemed to drown all noise and feeling.

"What?" his father screamed back, unable to hear above the rolling thunder.

Jacob felt as if he were trapped in a nightmare, the one where no matter how loud he tried to scream, no sound came out, or if it did, it emerged compressed and distorted, a static of meaningless noise. "Delaney!" he screamed, his face now directly before his father's, their dripping noses touching. "Delaney's dead!"

"Oh God!" Jacob heard his father say. "How? When?" he hollered.

"I don't know," Jacob shouted back, and began crying again.

"Come on, Richard! Let's go!" the other growers shouted. "It's getting worse!"

Jacob's father grabbed him by the hand, and as they came up behind the others, the group began moving through the storm. As they hurried, slipping in the mud toward the safety of home, Jacob turned his attention to the sky. The flashes were brighter than any light he had seen; his sight, which before had seemed indistinct, was sharpened by the intensity of the lightning. He winced as thin streaks of brilliance seared across his vision. Peering around him, he saw the backs of the other growers flashing in time with the light in the sky. Though the images remained blurry, he was amazed to discover he could see their heads distinct from their torsos and the movement of arms and legs. They all traveled together in a symmetry of fear. In the brilliant strobe he could see them duck downward in a collective crouch whenever the thunder crashed on them. They seemed to advance slowly, without real progress, as the erratic light revealed only fragments of their motion.

The landscape around him cast an eerie glow in the flashes and spread around him far into the distance, giving him his first visual awareness of the expansiveness of space. For a moment he forgot about death, forgot about danger, and was overwhelmed by the intensity of the experience, by the beauty of even the most awkward human movement, and by the smallness of human beings against the land's breadth. Suddenly a particularly strong bolt struck in front of him, flashed so close the thunder seemed to anticipate the lightning and explode before it was done flashing. The light seared his eyes, and for several seconds he could see nothing but the flash. In that moment he felt more terrified than he had ever felt before. He moved close to his father and clutched his hand tighter. It was only after they arrived home that he realized why he had been so afraid—he thought he had lost his sight for good.

The funeral was held two days later. Normally a funeral was a public event that most of Harmony attended, and it became, more or less, a Gathering. Standing on a small hilltop east of town, with people spread out below, Martin Corrow or some other council member would deliver a speech about the deceased, highlighting his contribution to the community, praising her loyalty to the ideals of Harmony and the Foundation. The deceased's sounder would then be presented to a loved one, its unique pitch forever a reminder of the one who had rejoined the greater darkness from which, Jacob had been taught, all things came. Afterward the citizens of Harmony who wished to do so could pay their last respects. Passing by the body in turn, people would trace their fingers across the face of the deceased to take away one last impression of their spouse, sibling, neighbor, or friend.

Jacob had attended many funerals but had made the final passing only once. Two years ago Delaney's mother, who had been ill for a long time, died, and Jacob made the trek to the body on the hilltop with his mother. At first Jacob was eager to make the passing; he had never touched a dead body before and was curious. As he stood in line, however, moving closer to the corpse of a woman he had met only a half dozen times in his life, he abruptly changed his mind. He quietly told his mother he wanted to leave, but she held him firmly by the shoulder and told him it was too late. "Everyone should experience death firsthand," she whispered. He could feel himself trembling as he approached the body. He reached out and moved his hand along the woman's face. He was surprised at the cold, smooth skin; it didn't feel like skin at all. Plastic and stiff, it left him feeling cold as well.

This funeral was different, however. Only a few people had been invited, and many in the community wondered at the high councilor's unusual decision. Yesterday many friends and neighbors of Jacob's family had stopped by to console his mother. She had hardly spoken since waking him with the news the previous night, and when she did speak, her voice sounded distant, so husky and strained that she seemed like a stranger to him. For a while he remained in the house with his parents as small groups arrived, speaking to her in hushed, sympathetic tones. Soon the ordeal became too much, and he felt like an intruder in the blackness of the underground home, an unwelcome witness to his mother's grief, which seemed to overwhelm his own.

He went outdoors to where a crowd gathered in the brightness of the street. It was a rest day—most people, aside from the growers, had no work—but the normal, relaxed tone that a rest day brought had disappeared. Everyone seemed tense and uneasy, and speculations whirled within the conversations. He listened to the people as they threw questions about, troubled by the mystery of the entire affair. Martin Corrow's announcement that morning that it would be a private ceremony—and that there would be no presentation of the body—puzzled many. Other questions surfaced too. How had she died? people wondered. Many thought suicide, but the idea of such an act was so disturbing that no one wanted to consider it, and Jacob knew no one in Harmony would dare ask. It seemed to be the only possibility to him, and he continued to feel a guilt so powerful that he couldn't begin to mention it to anyone, especially his parents.

Now gathered on the hill with his parents, Martin Corrow, and a few council members, Jacob relived, as he had repeatedly done in the last day and a half, his final conversation with the young woman, in which she had called him her friend. It seemed impossible that she could be gone. Without her here now, even in death, the ceremony seemed empty. It was as if they were saying good-bye to a stranger, as if someone else had died and Delaney had simply forgotten to join them in saying farewell. Her father recited a brief eulogy, praising his daughter's talent and her spirit, reminding them of their love for her.

"Though we will always remember her," he concluded, "we must all strive to continue our lives and forget the loss for the good of the community. I know Delaney would want that for us."

Jacob thought the farewell, in contrast to his usual eloquence, sounded hollow and didn't do justice to the truth of her life or death. Worse, it made *him* feel hollow, and that bothered him. Shouldn't he feel more? Funerals were common enough and had never affected him much before, but wasn't this different? Shouldn't he feel more sorrow? No. How could he? Why should he? She wasn't dead. He couldn't—wouldn't—accept it, and it made him angry to think that the others had, that her own father could so easily say good-bye.

When the high councilor had concluded, Jacob's mother played a song—one of her student's favorites—on the small harp she had brought. It was evening now, and as the notes from the harp lingered on the fading breeze, Jacob cast his eyes from the small crowd across to the horizon. He squinted into the distance. Though his vision was blurry, he discovered that with concentration, shapes consolidated and became more distinct. As he strained with the effort to gain control, contrasts in light and dark assumed a different tone as well. In addition to the globular light of the setting sun, he slowly found variations within the lighted forms about him. The rounded plains, no longer an undifferentiated dark mass, became a mixture of green and gold, colors that Jacob was seeing for the first time but could not name. And in the distance, against the dark trace of skyline, he could see a large mass rise up to brood on the horizon—his introduction to purple. He had learned about Nova Campi's two moons at school, as he had learned about the sun, and realized the blurry sphere must be one of them.

His eyes ached, but he didn't want to close them. These incredible differences in light added a whole new dimension to the vista, gave each component its own distinctiveness. Though the scene was still blurred, the richness of color endowed all parts with a depth so intense he could barely breathe at its splendor. He was shaking now. Was it from the pain of concentrated exertion or the power of the image? He held on, resisting the return to the moment. Was it the pulling away or the turning back that he hated most?

His strength gave out, and as the song continued, he closed his eyes to restrain the tears that welled up inside him. Though his eyes were closed to darkness once again, the landscape lingered in his awareness, and he resented himself for the awe he felt at its beauty. How could he feel that way about a world in which people failed one another constantly in large and little ways, a world in which Delaney was dead?

# PART TWO

# CHAPTER EIGHT

"Happy birthday, Jacob," his mother said, shaking him awake. It had been five days since the funeral, and things were returning to normal. This morning Jacob could hear a glimmer of his mother's former self in her voice. He knew she was making an effort to sound cheerful, perhaps against her own desire, but he was glad for the change anyway. Opening his eyes to utter blackness in the windowless underground house, Jacob stretched and sat up. His mother remained seated near the foot of his bed.

"Morning, Ma," he said.

"Thirteen. Hard to believe. How does it feel?"

"The same, I guess." Actually, it didn't, at least not when he considered how things had changed over the past few days. He recalled that morning, not even two weeks ago, when she had cut his hair. It seemed as if years had passed. Then he was still blind. Delaney was alive and still his mother's star pupil. Now he felt older. Not a better older, just older, waiting for further changes, more of the uncertainty that seemed to color every aspect of growing up.

"I remember when I turned thirteen," she said. "I don't know if I really felt older. Maybe fresher, like I was starting over, as though everything that had happened until that moment was part of somebody else's life, and now I was taking over. It was exciting. I had my music ahead of me, your father, you, but it was still out there, just waiting, and I didn't know anything about it. For the moment I was just fresh and in between." She finished talking and sat silently for a moment, reflecting.

Jacob understood what she was talking about in some ways but felt almost envious. He wished he could feel as if the past were another's life and that he was starting over. He didn't feel fresh. If anything, he felt stained, unclean from the accumulation of time.

"Your father told me to wish you happy birthday for him. His shift got switched to first, so he had to leave earlier than expected. But he'll join us tonight to celebrate. He was going to wake you up, but I insisted on letting you sleep in. After everything that's happened, you deserve a rest."

"You mean I'm not going to school today?" he asked.

"You can afford to miss a day. Did you want to go?"

"No, that's okay. I can stay home." He was too surprised to really be happy. After all, he had never missed a day of school.

"Good. Now, get dressed and come eat breakfast. I saved the last of the blackberry syrup for this morning. The flour's almost gone, but there should be enough for a few decent pancakes."

He arose, lingering in his room, taking time to dress. He listened to her making pancakes in the kitchen, listened to the clanging pans, the whisking of tin on tin. Entering the kitchen at last, he took his seat and found she had already set the dishes. A cloth placemat, used for special occasions, lay beneath the chipped plate. The fork and knife, slightly warped by use, lay next to it, wrapped also in cloth—one of the good napkins.

"Quite the royal treatment this morning, Ma," he commented.

"You deserve it, Jake," she said, then hesitated. "I know it's been tough these last few days, but things will improve. You'll see."

He gasped, and a quick surge ran through him at her last words. Such expressions were frowned upon in Harmony, almost heretical, but people still slipped from time to time. But the more personal meaning of her words was what struck him. She couldn't know, could she? Of course not; it was just an innocent slip. "You know what I mean," she added quickly, her voice dropping in embarrassment.

She sighed and slipped the hot pancakes onto his plate. He covered them with syrup and took a mouthful. He ate the entire meal quickly while she sat across from him at the table. They remained silent. He tried to savor the rich sweetness of the syrup, the last of a delicacy that might not be replaced for some time, but he was too nervous to truly enjoy the experience. *Maybe I should tell her,* he thought. No. It wasn't the right time. It was too soon after everything that had happened. She didn't deserve to be hit with this, especially on his birthday and after she had treated him to this special breakfast, had kept him home from school. To say anything else, to initiate the lightest of conversation, however, seemed like just another form of deception, and so he said nothing.

"Finished? So quickly," she said.

"I was hungry," he replied. "I think I'll go outside."

"Oh," she said. He could hear the disappointment. "I was hoping you would stay with me awhile. I thought we might play together. I have a new composition and could use your help. Besides, it wouldn't be a good idea for you to wander too much when you're supposed to be in school. If somebody heard you, there might be questions."

"All right," he agreed, even though he was certain no one would detect him. He hadn't played with her for a while, and perhaps it might lift her spirits.

"Great," she said, brightening. Together they cleaned up the table, washed the dishes, and then sat at the piano. Jacob took the lower keys, while she played the upper registers. To warm up, she picked a song they had played together often—one of her own compositions. Things began well enough, but as they progressed further into the song, Jacob found himself feeling more and more distracted. He kept thinking about the colors and shapes that had been filling his consciousness for the last several days, the deep blue of the sky, the stretching green of the plains, and the dark forms of prairie birds soaring back and forth between these two realms. He began making mistakes, forgetting chords and measures, plunking the wrong keys, creating awkward dissonances that spoiled the song. Try as he might, he couldn't dispel the images from his mind. With each new mistake he began wondering if this was what sight did to a person, if this was why they had turned away from it. His teachers had often referred to the shallow distractions of appearances—maybe this was what they meant. Several times they had to stop altogether and start a section over, much to his frustration and, he could tell, hers too. When they finally reached the end, she didn't hold the sustain pedal as the composition called for, but released it abruptly, cutting off the last chord, leaving a vacuum of sound to match her stillness.

"I'm not feeling very musical today," he told her. "I'm sorry."

She didn't respond. He got up from the piano bench and slipped away, back to his room, guilty for leaving. For the next several hours they avoided each other in the pitch-blackness of the windowless house. He wandered in and out of his room, fighting back the urge to get out, away from the dark and into the light he found himself steadily craving. She, in turn, stayed mostly at the piano, working on a composition. He recognized the piece. It was one she had begun writing with Delaney only a few weeks ago.

Finally he could stand it no longer. He came up behind his mother, now silent at the bench, and tapped her shoulder, feeling her startle at his touch.

"I'm going out," he said. "I promised Egan we'd get together after school today."

"It's early yet," she said. When he didn't answer, she sighed. "Fine, have a nice time. Just stay out of trouble, okay?"

"I will," he said, turning for the door. Before he could get away, she reached out and grabbed his arm in the darkness and pulled him to her. She held him for a moment, her arms tight around his waist, her head against his chest. He stood there with his arms at his sides, allowing her to hold him. After a minute she released him silently. He squeezed her shoulder lightly and left, closing the door quietly behind him.

The day was beautiful. Shining down from a blue, cloudless sky, the sun illuminated the streets and hillsides. He could see more clearly now, more so since the funeral when he had watched the moon rise over the plains. He could navigate almost exclusively by sight and marveled at the freedom it brought him. He wondered if his eyes now showed him what the Seers saw. As he wandered through the Impressionist painting of his vision, avoiding the shadowy figures of the occasional passerby, moving ever faster through the streets, he soon forgot the darkness of the house and the awkward scene with his mother. He forgot about everything—his birthday, specialization, the fight between his parents at dinner yesterday for the second night in a row. Best of all, he forgot about Delaney. Though the reality of her death had steadily begun to sink in, part of him still couldn't believe she was gone, and that same sick feeling rose inside when he remembered her voice, her laugh. By now everyone understood her death to be suicide, though no one wanted to discuss it.

Instead he lingered by the fountains in the squares, watching the sparkles that the water created in the sunlight as it gushed into the pools. He spoke to no one and avoided others by ducking down empty side streets, resting in the shade amid the neighborhood flower beds and herb gardens when the brightness of noon dazzled his vision. Buzzing among the purple and yellow flowers, only the insects that browsed on nectar seemed to notice him. The afternoon passed slowly this way as Jacob explored. It was strange walking by sight through the community. He had grown up in Harmony, had traversed virtually every street and lane, yet it felt like a different place now. Defined by the boundaries of form, it seemed smaller than it had in darkness, where no horizon existed, where distance was measured more in time than space. Perhaps it had shrunk because he could cover ground more quickly, or perhaps it was because the uniformity of gray buildings and identical rows of hillhouses made every part of town seem the same. The symmetry of the settlement that made navigation simple and provided a comforting predictability in blindness had begun, over the last few days, to impose a bland rigidity on Jacob's world.

People were different. The indistinct figures he encountered always gave him pause. Previously, in his blindness, others he passed in the street would come and go, an anonymous part of the environment. Now, however, safe in the knowledge that he couldn't be seen, he became a watcher, wondering about the identity of each person. Who were the indistinguishable shapes that passed him in the street? How were they connected to him? The mystery added a thrill to his voyeurism and provided moving obstacles in his exploration. Though he wore his sounder, he would step out of range before a stranger came too close. He felt as if he were playing the hider in a child's game of seeker that no one around him knew they played.

Then, in the middle of his wanderings, he stopped. He thought of his mother sitting alone in the house, playing a song that no one heard but her. A fresh wave of guilt washed over him. He thought of the breakfast she had made him, how she had given him the best of what they had, how she had brightened when he agreed to play piano with her. And how did he repay her? By fleeing as quickly as he could to run around the streets of Harmony, playing games in secret. He suddenly felt selfish. Even if it was his birthday, it was wrong to put his desires before others, especially her. Maybe he was becoming a Seer after all, was becoming everything he had been taught to disdain. Closing his eyes, he wondered, *Am I a bad person?*

His mood darkened, in spite of the sun, as he found his way to school and waited until the students were released. He watched them leave, clusters of walking figures separating into blurry groups. Homing in on the pitch of his friend's sounder, he intercepted Egan as he left the school yard.

Egan greeted him with his usual humor. "So, you've come, raised up from your deathbed." He paused, suddenly awkward at the mention of death. "I mean, they told us you were sick today."

"Not really. My mother let me stay home from school. It's my birthday, remember?"

"Oh, right," Egan said in mock forgetfulness. "How old are you again?"

"Shut up," Jacob said, pushing him. They both laughed. It felt good to laugh with his friend again. The last few days had been dulled not only by Delaney's death, but also by Egan's uncharacteristic silence. Jacob's suspicions about Mr. Spencer had been correct. Egan had been forced to stay by his father's side during the delivery and listen to an old recording of a Francis Aldrich lecture on Truesight. Jacob knew Egan felt guilty about not meeting him and tried repeatedly to counter Egan's apologies. He said nothing to his friend about what really happened. Instead he told Egan that he had waited for him at school for a while and then returned home. In fact, Jacob felt relieved that his friend hadn't shown up. Things might have been worse than they were.

"I figured you weren't really sick anyway—your mother's a softy. I hope you appreciate how lucky you are. My parents made me go to school on my thirteenth birthday last month." Jacob didn't respond to his friend's joking play for sympathy. Though neither one fully acknowledged it, they both knew Egan, with his father's connections, had it easier.

"What do you want to do?" Jacob said instead. "I don't have to be home until dinner."

"I know—let's head over to the north field and go for a run."

"Sounds good to me. You know I'm just going to beat you again."

"Doubt it. I've been practicing."

They headed toward the outskirts of Harmony through the north end of town, where the settlement ended abruptly. Unlike the southern end of the colony, which was developed into large squares of cultivated earth for crops, and the eastern edge, where cattle and sheep grazed, the north end was just a broad expanse of grass. Originating behind the last tier of hillhouses, the field extended several hundred yards to the perimeter of the colony, where a line of pathminders circled the outer edge, curving around to create a border no one ever crossed. The council had erected the perimeter several years ago after a child wandered off while playing and disappeared into the plains. Though her sounder was found not far from Harmony, the girl was never heard from again. With the pathminders in place—the only outer section of the colony to be so enclosed—the area was designated for recreation and had since become popular with the colony's children. It was a nice spot to get away from their parents and neighbors, and the two boys sometimes went there to play.

Starting from the hilltop, they would have a race, plowing blindly into the tall grass and running as fast as they could to hear whose sounder would be triggered by the bordering pathminders first. Jacob sometimes wondered what would happen if they continued to the other side, into the open plains, but he had never dared find out, and even Egan never raised the possibility of committing such a bold transgression. Instead they always stopped short and quickly moved back until their sounders were silent again, as if the guilty noise itself would give them away. A little larger than his friend, Jacob usually won these races, but not always; part of the challenge was moving as quickly as possible without tripping in the tall grass, because one fall could mean victory for the other. Still, it wasn't really winning that was important about these races, at least not to Jacob—Egan was more competitive and took defeat closer to heart—it was really about the freedom that came with running, of being able to hurl yourself into the unknown and not care about what happened. It was the only time he ever felt that way.

Now they stood on the grassy roof of the last house in the northern tier, each bracing for the race. Egan, as always, performed the honors.

"Ready. Set." He paused, relishing the suspense. "Go!" he shouted.

They took off down the hill, bounding into the grassy field. Jacob whooped with a joyful cry that caught him by surprise as he plunged into the green expanse dotted with the gold of prairie flowers, aiming for the horizon, where green met the blue of sky. Egan was a dark blur to his right, on the periphery and slowly dropping from sight. He ran faster, his breath coming in quick gasps. The added dimensions of shape and color brought a beauty to the flow of movement and simultaneously removed some of the thrill of the run, a thrill that came from traveling through unknown blackness so carelessly. He closed his eyes and felt the thrill return.

When he opened his eyes again, he saw the blurry figure of Egan now in front of him and moving swiftly ahead. Trying to regain ground, Jacob ran harder, speeding up until he could almost touch the white back of his friend's shirt. Then he was falling into grass, tumbling into blackness as his eyes shut themselves instinctively with the plunge. He hit the ground squarely, rolling over in a tangle of stalks and flowers and coming to a stop. For a while he lay there with his eyes closed, gasping for the breath that had been knocked out of him. Lying on his back, trying to take deep breaths to fill his lungs, he remembered the first time—the only other occasion—he had had the wind knocked out of him. He had fallen down while playing at recess during the first week of school. The suffocating feeling terrified him and he cried for his teacher, convinced he was dying. After the teacher had calmed him and his wind had returned, she chastised him harshly, telling him— and all the other students gathered to listen—that he should have been more careful, that that's what came from rushing, from denying the reality of his blindness and believing he could move so capriciously.

He rolled over and opened his eyes. They opened to a crystal world. His mind exploded at the crispness of everything around him. He could see the texture of every blade of grass, the detail of each flower in front of him. Looking skyward, he could see the perfect blue marred only by the faintest wisp of high cumulus clouds. He closed his eyes once more and took a deep breath. Only then did he realize that he had been waiting for this moment forever, and he knew that this was what it meant to truly see. He dared not open his eyes. What if this perfection had disappeared? Then he couldn't stand the suspense and opened them. Everything was still as it was a moment ago. He looked once more into the grass and saw an insect before him, perched on the thick purple stalk of a flower. No, there were two of them, he noticed as he leaned closer. The larger one, attached to the stalk, glistening yellow and black and measuring the length of his palm, gripped a smaller one between forelegs almost equal in length to its thorax. The spiky black legs securely held the struggling pale green insect, which jerked wildly in a futile attempt to escape. Jacob watched, transfixed, as the larger bug proceeded to bite with giant mandibles into the head of its prey, which quickly stopped thrashing, giving only a few involuntary spasms as it became food for its captor.

The insects, coupled together in a spectacle of predator and prey, disappeared beneath the foot that came crashing down in front of Jacob's face. A pair of legs parted the grass.

"No!" Jacob shouted in horror.

"Jacob?" Egan said wildly. "Are you okay?"

"I'm fine," Jacob blurted out, rising to his feet. He stared at his friend, who now stood before him, marveling at the detail. He had touched the faces of people, including his friend, and had noted the subtle differences in features that identified every individual, but to see the human face in its entirety amazed him. Egan's cropped brown hair, small nose, and thin lips were eerily familiar, yet pulled together and seen as a whole, along with the light green eyes, unsettled Jacob. It was as if his friend had suddenly been transformed into a stranger.

"What's going on? Didn't you hear me calling you?" Egan was worried. Jacob could tell by his voice and now could see it in the narrowed brow, the tightened lips.

"I'm sorry," Jacob said. He wanted to grab his friend and tell him about the miracle, tell him everything that had happened to him, but when he tried, something prevented him. "I just had the wind knocked out of me."

"Oh. That's all? Well, too bad, then, because clearly you were too incapacitated to hear me win." Egan's worried frown now converted to a smile. Jacob realized he was busy watching his friend's face again and barely listening to his words.

"You just got lucky," he finally conceded, hastily trying to cover for the long, awkward pause.

"Are you sure you didn't hit your head also? You sound funny." Egan didn't bother to wait for a response to the rhetorical jab at his friend. "Anyway, I didn't get lucky. I was way ahead of you even before you fell."

"You were," Jacob agreed.

Before his eyes Egan's face, the tall field grass, the clouds, all disappeared, reverting to a blur of color and indistinct shapes. In a moment the clarity was gone, and he was struck by a pang of disappointment. Again, as he had at the funeral, he squinted in concentration, and after several seconds the world responded like the settling of a pool, returning to focus, bringing a rush that set his heart pounding once more. They walked back toward the settlement, where they could hear wind chimes in the distance.

"Egan, do you ever feel different?" he asked tentatively.

"Yes. Earlier today, in school, I was sad because I was bored, and now I'm happy because I'm not." He laughed. Jacob didn't; he was attempting to be serious and grew mildly annoyed at his friend's unwillingness to engage in real conversation.

"No. I mean different from everyone else. Like you're not like other people."

"No one's the same, Jacob."

"I know no one's the same. You like some things; I like other things. But I guess I mean in another way. Like in a bad way. Like you're too different. Like you're only waiting for the time when everyone will suddenly notice, and then it's too late."

"Too late for what?"

"I don't know. Too late to change. Too late to be normal."

"I don't know what you're talking about, Jacob." Egan sounded annoyed, frustrated. "Hey, are you trying to say there's something wrong with me? Is this because you lost the race?"

"No . . . of course not," Jacob stammered. *Typical, Egan*, he thought. *It's always about you.*

"Well, there's nothing wrong with me. I'm fine, okay?" He sounded less angry now and spoke reassuringly.

"I know you are. You always have been. Forget it."

"Is it about her?" Egan asked, as if he were unable to say the name.

"No, it's not about Delaney. Like I said, forget it. I'm not even sure what I'm talking about. I think you're right; I must have hit my head back there." They walked for a while in silence, pausing near the turnoff for Egan's street.

"Just remember, that's why we're here, in Harmony. Everyone is joined together by a single way of life. We aren't that different from one another; we don't have to be. We all have each other and that's what's nice about it," Egan said. Jacob managed to stifle a laugh at his friend's characteristic mock solemnity; he sounded like Mrs. Lawson from civics class. Only after Egan had left did Jacob realize his friend had been totally sincere.

# CHAPTER NINE

"Why are we eating up here again, Jacob?" Richard Manford asked his son.

"I don't know. I just felt like it," Jacob said quietly.

"Leave him alone, Richard," Jacob's mother chided. "It's his birthday."

Jacob looked at his mother, marveling at the wholeness of her face. Her long hair, so blond it was almost white, was pulled tightly into a long ponytail, held in place by a piece of frayed string. The hair cascaded down her back all the way to her waist, fanning out into strands that were picked up and floated by the evening breeze from time to time. Though dressed in a simple robe, its tan folds gathered around her as she sat cross-legged on the grass, she nonetheless exuded a lightness, from the delicacy of her small features all the way to the tips of her long, thin fingers. He had always known she was a small woman, but to see her clearly to such a degree, down to the individual eyelashes, so light they were almost transparent, unsettled him. Though Jacob found her face, her entire body, pleasing in its delicate symmetry, he also found that it seemed to diminish her, to reduce her to this physical form that wasn't much larger than he was.

Looking at his father, he was startled by the contrast. He was as large as he'd seemed the few times Jacob had felt the muscular arms and back, perhaps even larger. He was a man shaped by labor. Jacob could see the hands, hardened, covered with little scars, still darkened with soil and machine oil that never completely washed away but lingered in the crevices, highlighting fingernails and knuckles. Though not unhandsome, his facial features were rough and craggy, with a large nose and deep-set eyes. His entire head, including his shaved scalp, was a uniform tan from days spent in the fields, unlike his willowy mother, who spent most of her time indoors. They were night and day, these two people who had given him life, though both seemed much thinner than Egan, despite his father's wiry bulk. Their faces conveyed a leanness in the slightly sunken cheekbones that Jacob found mildly disturbing.

He looked beyond both of them and at the ground in front of him. The cloth that normally covered the dinner table now lay spread across the short grass that doubled as the roof of their home. It was weighted down with plates, flatware, and bowls of food, and its edges flapped in the breeze in time with his mother's hair. The meal before them was a veritable feast. His father had smuggled some fresh beans from one of the fields he worked in—desperately warning Jacob not to tell anyone, even Egan, especially Egan—and his mother had managed to acquire some meat, several scrawny but still delicious chicken legs. She wouldn't say where she'd gotten them.

Turning his gaze up and away, he looked beyond his parents. The grassy ridge that covered his house, and the houses of everyone on his street, was one of the highest in the colony. Right in the middle of the North Tier, not far from the fountain in the square, it afforded him a broad view of Harmony. Aside from a few of the larger structures—some of which Jacob guessed to be the school, the council house, and the larger store-houses in the western area of the settlement—much of the town seemed indistinguishable from the surrounding plains. The homes, camouflaged beneath the grassy waves of ridges and hills, were nearly invisible, aside from a few western-facing metallic house fronts in the eastern tier that glittered as they reflected light from the setting sun. Otherwise, it was hard to tell where Harmony began and where the outside world took over, stretching out to the horizon in layer upon layer of grasslands.

Jacob scanned the entire horizon, absorbing the clarity, not knowing how long it would last. Several times after he'd left Egan, his vision had blurred, but he found that with blinking and concentrated squinting, he could refocus, each time more quickly and with greater ease, until finally his vision seemed to hold and hadn't wavered. The sun sat low in the west, reduced from the blinding spot above him in the heat of noon to a small white disk that seemed tired and sullen, having spent its daily quota of energy and light. In the south the fields formed dark squares, covering an area almost as large as the rest of the settlement itself. But Jacob found his gaze hurrying past them to the east, where the real spectacle was unfolding. He had seen the moon rise five days before at the funeral. Then it had been a blob of dim purple light. Now it stood in high definition, halfway over the plains and so vast it seemed to fill the entire eastern sky. What struck him most were the rings. Rising at a forty-five-degree angle to the horizon, the multicolored bands formed a sliver that sliced the purple of the moon itself and formed a thin, oblong disk that seemed to bisect the sphere it contained. Along this sliver Jacob could see clusters of sparkles scattered across the velvet circle of rings.

Jacob found himself overwhelmed. He didn't know which way to gaze, what to watch—the splendor of the vista or the intricacies of detail immediately surrounding him? It was almost too much. Too much beauty, too much stimulation. He wanted to close his eyes but was afraid he might lose clarity. He craved the clear sight that seemed so long in coming. He wanted it to remain, in spite of the pangs of guilt that gnawed at the edges of his desire. *How can this be wrong?* he wondered, thinking back to his earlier doubts. All his life he had been told that what he was doing now was wrong, corrupt, led to pain and suffering. But it seemed like all he had been feeling for the last two weeks was suffering, and now the only anodyne was the moon, the horizon, and the forms of his mother and father, even the chipped plates and dull knives on the frayed tablecloth. On the other hand, these past two weeks had coincided with the arrival of his sight, and with each passing day, with every hour since clarity had come, he could feel himself pulling away, pulling away, like the rounded corner of the moon now severing itself from the horizon's edge.

"Well, I like it up here," his mother chirped. "The breeze is lovely, and listen to those birds. Their music is as beautiful as any of ours." Her blue eyes, as pale as her blond hair, stared blankly ahead as she spoke, but her lips worked into a smile, though the smile faded as soon as she stopped talking. He tuned his ears to where a pair of prairie birds sang on the ridge below and across from them. He watched them flutter in an intricate dance as their cries intertwined, a series of dramatic staccato peeps that rose and sank quickly into the low wail of a drawn-out coo. He wondered why they were dancing.

"I didn't say I didn't like it," his father responded. "I was just curious why Jacob wanted to eat outside. Not that I mind it out here. After all, I spend all day outside, rain or shine, hot or cold. I've grown quite used to it." Jacob watched his father's face contort, accentuating only the slightest sarcasm in his voice that Jacob might otherwise have missed. The raised eyebrows and tight smile transformed him, made him a stranger to his son.

His mother didn't respond, though she must have sensed his tone, since Jacob observed the anger in her face. The drawn eyebrows and pursed lips created as startling an image as his father's sarcastic face had, and a visible coldness seemed to wash over her, not dousing the anger, but enhancing its power. Then it passed and a quick smile returned.

"This reminds me of when you were younger, Jacob. We used to have picnics all the time. Remember, Richard?" Her voice retained its sweetness, but her smile, like his father's before, became a sneer.

*What does she mean?* Jacob wondered. His father didn't answer but scowled.

"I remember, Ma," Jacob said softly. The unfolding spectacle unnerved him. It was as if there were two conversations occurring. He would never have guessed how much people communicated through their faces and bodies. He was both repulsed by and curious at his parents' behavior. "This is good chicken, Ma. Where'd you say you got it again?" He could see her stiffen at the question. A look of concern crossed her face.

"Didn't we already discuss this? It's a secret, a special arrangement for your birthday." Jacob watched her head tilt down and her eyes blink as she spoke. Her thin smile came and went almost as quickly.

"Jacob, stop teasing your mother," his father put in. "She obviously doesn't want to ruin the surprise. Just enjoy the chicken, and those beans I risked my neck to get for you."

Jacob had no idea what was transpiring. *Why is he defending her all of a sudden?* Jacob wondered. This entire drama that neither of them knew he could see both baffled and angered him. He felt like a fool. Was every meal this way? He suddenly didn't want to know. Instead he watched their faces—his mother's cold and angry, his father's cautious and sad. Jacob's eyes lowered, following his father's rough hand as it reached over and touched his mother's leg. She quickly grabbed his hand and pushed it away. Jacob watched her turn her head away from her husband, almost as if her blank eyes could see.

"By the way, Jake," she said, "your father and I have a present for you."

Jacob saw her remove a small object from the pocket of her robe. She moved in his direction, reaching her hand out tentatively in an effort to find him. He intercepted her, taking the gift from her hand. It was a small metallic cube with a tiny handle attached to its side. He immediately knew what it was—another music box to replace the one he had destroyed. But this one was different: it was larger, heavier, and engraved with intricate designs pleasing to the touch, a more sophisticated version of the unadorned toy he had been given eight years ago. When he opened the lid, however, the same familiar tune began to play—a child's song about planted children who were never plucked from their flower beds. He closed the lid quickly, cutting off the tune midnote.

# CHAPTER TEN

Jacob looked below at the storage houses. The half dozen structures sat in a neat block at the western edge of town. Square and squat, nearly perfect cubes of steel, they contrasted with the random assortment of hills behind them that comprised most of the town. On the outer perimeter of the buildings the land flattened, easing into gentle rises that formed a great plain, before rising up into a disappearing sequence of hilly ridges in the distance. It was midafternoon, and the students had been dismissed an hour ago in preparation for a Gathering. It was the second day after his birthday, and for the second day Jacob did not go home after school. Instead he went exploring.

Yesterday, before Egan had a chance to talk to him, Jacob had immediately left and struck out by himself. He had wandered around the eastern tier of Harmony, meandering through the streets that lay between the rows of hillhouses until reaching the edge of town. There, the terrain flattened—as on the western and southern sides, though not as much—into pastureland, where he watched the animals graze. Cattle were in one field. He had visited the small barns nearby when he was younger, listening then as the cattle tenders acquainted him and his father with the work of feeding and milking the cows, and the challenge of slaughtering the bulls and the occasional older cow when beef was needed. He had also met the sheep tenders, who allowed him to feel the woolly backs of the animals that provided much of the community's clothing, and meat as well. He remembered being frightened of the animals, especially the larger cattle, whose massive sides disappeared above his highest reach and whose heavy, snorting breath felt hot against his face. One of the cows had knocked him down, leaning over him with a wet muzzle to lick his face. He was shaken but determined not to cry, and his father praised him for his composure.

Yesterday, however, returning to the edge of the pasture, he had been surprised at how different the cattle appeared. They still seemed large, especially in comparison with the people he had seen, but in the field they seemed less intimidating, tranquilly grazing or lying about. They had no cares or worries. They watched him, too, as he approached. He felt uneasy for a moment and conspicuous, as if the staring animals possessed some secret power to tell their human masters his secret. But their empty stares, devoid of interest, soon made him feel foolish at the thought.

One of the cows that grazed nearby eventually approached him as he stood silently. He retreated as she moved to the edge of the pathminders, her signal collar preventing her from moving any farther. For a moment they stared at each other. He was amazed at the size of the docile eyes; they were huge, reflective, almost kind. It felt good to see a creature that saw him back, and at that moment he felt closer to the animal than to any human being; at least the cow saw the world the way he saw it, shared with him the consciousness of light. She bent down and pulled a tuft of grass, chewing it with enormous molars, crunching it with a grinding sound pleasant to his ears. Then she sauntered away, left him standing there alone.

He went over to the sheep pasture. The scene was more or less identical, though the sheep were huddled together more closely, moving as a single unit as they browsed among the grass. Several of them were softly lowing as they grazed, their bleating forming a disjointed melody, and he was reminded for a moment of the weekly Gatherings in the main square.

There was a Gathering today—right now, in fact—

but he was not present. Instead he found himself back on that hilltop behind the storage houses, where only a week ago he had encountered Delaney for the last time. He wasn't certain why he had returned, but he had. It felt strange not to be at a Gathering and to stare at the deserted paths and buildings while everyone was collected in the middle of Harmony. But it would have felt stranger to be there, surrounded by every person in the colony, blindly herded together in the square, and he remembered the claustrophobic panic that had paralyzed him at the last one.

He pulled up a tuft of grass and examined it, looking at the purple stems and green blades. The tips were seeded, each one encased in hairy fibers and gathered into sheaths. He stripped one of the sheaths away, pulling against the grain until all the seeds were collected in his cupped palm. Each one lay separate and distinct, little tear-shaped pods of life all from a single stem. He blew into his hand and the seeds scattered, jumping out, then disappearing into the covered ground. He tore the empty stem in half, threw it away, and closed his eyes against his sight. Why had it happened to him? What was he supposed to do with it? How long would he, or could he, live alone with the secret, and what would happen to him once it was discovered? There had to be some meaning behind what was happening, but he couldn't figure out what it was. That was why he'd come to this spot, he realized. He hoped that coming here might allow him time to think, that by returning to the place where he'd left Delaney, he might find her here again, or at least a part of her spirit that could give him the strength to make sense of it all. He hoped that as the outer world was made clear, some inner truth might be revealed. But returning revealed nothing but an awareness of his own futility.

He pulled another tuft, listening to the ripping sound made by the fibers as he tore the grass away. It reminded him of the cow he had seen yesterday. He remembered the connection he had felt with the animals. He was one of them, dull, passive, just a watcher standing back against the current of the world. No, they were better. At least they lived their days in relative peace, unconcerned with the future, oblivious to time. They had no secrets or lies. He had lied to his mother this morning in the lightless house, telling her he was attending the Gathering with Egan. She had accepted his lie without a word, and he had fled the darkness with a mixture of relief and shame.

*Maybe Egan was right. Maybe I do think too much,* he told himself. A quiet voice spoke up, told him he must worry less and enjoy the gift of his sight. The thought startled him. Then another voice chastised him. *It is not a gift*, it said. *It is a curse. You are cursed.* He lay back in the cushion of grass and stared at the clouds that had been rolling in over the last hour, covering up the sun and darkening the plains. Which voice was really his?

A loud bang and the sound of creaking metal made him sit up. He crawled forward a few yards and looked below through the parted grass. The door of the storehouse closest to him was open, the padlock broken. A steel rod leaned against the wall next to the door. Watching carefully, Jacob made his way down the hill, remaining in the deep grass at the edge of the clearing, now only a dozen yards from the building. A minute passed, and then another. He watched, scarcely moving, hardly breathing.

A third minute passed before a man appeared in the doorway. Jacob instinctively crouched to hide before realizing the man couldn't see him. He stood up to get a better look. The man, tall with graying hair, his face gaunt with hollow cheeks and eyes, hurried from the building, stopping briefly to cock his head and listen for any sounds that might indicate a threat. Jacob noticed he was carrying an armful of food—several loaves of bread and some other, unknown packages of foodstuffs. Without thinking, Jacob followed the man to town along the main road. Soon they were back in the settlement proper, hurrying among streets. The man evaded the main avenue that led to the central square where everyone had convened. At one point he stopped and turned, his wide eyes pointing in Jacob's direction. The boy froze immediately, his heart pounding at the thought of discovery. After several seconds of silence, the man continued.

As he followed the man through a maze of streets, Jacob's body trembled at the sight. He was now not only witnessing a crime—perhaps one of the most serious crimes possible in Harmony—but was actually following the thief home. True, his father had stolen some beans from the field, but a handful of smuggled vegetables seemed a far cry from the bounty this man carried in his arms, a bounty taken directly from the storehouse that held the community's dwindling food supply. The armful seemed the equivalent of an entire week's worth of rations. He had never heard of such a theft occurring. An alarming thought struck him: Was he seeing something occurring for the first time, or had such crimes happened before? Maybe he should report the man, cry out and reveal him. But that would also mean revealing himself. Besides, no one was nearby, the streets were empty. Jacob decided to follow the thief home, find out who he was, and then decide.

The man stopped one more time. He seemed to be

slowing his pace and breathing heavily. Jacob watched as he set the armful down. The man removed a folded piece of gray cloth from his shirt and held it against his mouth and nose, as if he were about to smother himself. Then, bending over, he coughed sporadically into the cloth. Jacob saw his back heave as spasms shook his body. The man made hardly a sound, however, carefully muffling the noise in his rag. Jacob then knew his identity, who the man must be. He knew only one man who coughed like that, who made that terrible sound—Tobin Fletcher, who lived at the end of Jacob's street and who worked as one of the storehouse keepers.

When his coughing spasm subsided, Tobin placed the cloth in his pocket and, hastily gathering the food, scurried down the street. Jacob resumed following him, but as he passed the spot where the man had paused, he noticed a cardboard box on the ground. It had fallen away from the pile, and Tobin hadn't missed it. Jacob picked it up. The box was small—about six by ten inches—but heavy. He wondered what was in it, but there was no time to open it now. He needed to follow the man home, to make certain it was really him. Sure enough, they passed through the western tier and into the northern section of town. They crossed the fountain square and soon came to the street they shared. Jacob stopped before his own door, following the thief with his eyes until he disappeared inside his neighboring house.

Jacob entered and took the box to his room. He hesitated before opening it. Wouldn't that make him an accomplice to the crime? Could he reveal it to anyone without having to explain himself? Jacob wasn't certain that he should. Though he was horrified by the blatant theft he had witnessed, an act that went against everything he had been taught, he actually liked Tobin. He also felt sorry for the poor man. Both he and his wife, Penny, had been ill for some time. Several of the people in their tier, including his parents once or twice, had helped them on occasion, covering for Tobin when he was unable to work his shift, or helping Penny with work when she was too weak to get out of bed. The Fletchers' next-door neighbor had even discreetly taken up a collection last week, going door to door for any extra food they might spare (which was little) in the hopes that it might improve Penny's strength and, ultimately, her health. Now, with the recently reduced rations, maybe they really needed the food. Maybe their lives depended on it. Did that make what he saw wrong? Did that make it right?

Either way, he decided he couldn't reveal his neighbor's theft. He opened the box carefully. His mother wasn't home, probably at the Gathering, but he still felt the need to be quiet, as if she could hear him across town. Reaching in the carton, he fumbled in the darkness. The box was packed with a dozen small cans. He removed one of the cool, smooth cylinders and, pulling the tab, opened the lid. He sniffed its contents, and a familiar smell struck him. Pears. He had had the fruit only a couple times in his life, on special occasions, but their taste had left an impression on him. He hurried to the kitchen for a spoon and headed back to his room. Then he dove into the can, gobbling down the sweet, slippery fruit neatly sliced into halves. When he had finished, he drank the light syrup until nothing remained. He replaced the cover and put the empty can in the box, resisting the urge to eat every single container of fruit, deciding to save them for later.

That evening, at dinner, his parents talked about the Gathering.

"I think the high councilor gave a particularly good speech today, don't you, Richard?" she said.

"Absolutely. People need to be reassured about the harvest," Richard said. "Tomorrow we'll be able to start processing the crops for storage, and in a week or two things should be back to normal. I've heard too much grumbling lately, and frankly, I'm starting to get tired of it."

"But people are hungry, aren't they?" Jacob asked him.

"Of course. We all are, a little. The last month has been hard; we all realize that, but people aren't starving, are they? Are you starving, Jacob?"

"I guess not," he answered.

"Of course not. Nobody's ever starved, and nobody ever will. That's why it bothers me so much, the quiet complaining. That's not in the spirit of Harmony, like the high councilor said today."

"Maybe it's harder on some people than on others," Jacob said.

"Why should it be? Everyone gets the same amount of food," his father said.

"How do you know they do?" Jacob asked.

"How do I know? Because that's the way things are around here. How do you know they don't? That's the real question, Jacob."

"Egan told me his family had a roast the other night. How did they get that?" he challenged.

"Egan's family is bigger than ours. Besides, maybe they didn't accept their meat ration last month. They might have been saving it for this month. Did you ask him?"

"No, I didn't."

"There you go. Jacob, everyone knows that some people in Harmony get special privileges once in a while, councilors and such. It's no secret. But they have greater responsibilities. It's only fair. But when it comes to food, everyone is treated the same. Didn't they teach you that in school?"

"Yes," Jacob answered weakly.

"I know they did. I learned the same things when I went to school. Hey, all I'm trying to say is that we take care of one another. Except for a very few things, we don't depend on the Seers for our sustenance. That's what makes us unique. It's what makes us pure. Hardship is good for the soul. It keeps us honest."

Jacob asked to be excused and went to his room. He opened another can of pears and ate them before going to bed. They were delicious but not quite as wonderful as before; their sweetness seemed diminished after the conversation with his father, their flavor tinged with a mixture of guilt and cynicism. He had always believed his father's words, his teachers' comments. But today he hadn't seen much honesty or, remembering the lean image of the hunched and coughing Tobin, much purity either.

# CHAPTER ELEVEN

The next morning, on a rise at the edge of the fields, Jacob sat and watched the growers, busy with the work of harvesting. He glanced nervously as men and women moved about, calling instructions to one another, wheeling carts of newly harvested vegetables from the edges of the crops to the great bins that would carry them to the storehouses for processing. It was late morning, and the sun shone hot. He could see the sweat on the workers as they passed him, drops running off their brows and staining their tunics in dark patches. Occasionally they stopped for water, but for the most part they worked steadily, moving back and forth along the rows, feeling for ripeness, filling their baskets.

He was supposed to be in school, but that morning, right before he entered the dark building, he had paused and stepped aside as the others moved ahead. Nobody noticed. Since leaving the house that morning, he had debated whether or not to skip. At the last moment, the idea of spending the next four hours in the darkness of the classroom seemed too dismal, especially after yesterday's events. The theft continued to bother him, as did his father's words at dinner. He decided instead to go to the fields where his father worked. His father had mentioned they would begin harvesting today, and he wanted to see it happen. He figured it would be as educational as anything he would learn that day, especially in Mrs. Lawson's class. Besides, school was nearing the end, and in a few more days everyone would be joining the growers in the fields, carefully combing the crops to make sure nothing was wasted. Tomorrow and the next day he would have final tests, which he dare not miss; today would be his last and only chance to skip out. He figured he would probably get in trouble, but he didn't care.

When he first arrived at the fields, he walked around, quietly shadowing the growers as they engaged in their separate tasks. Soon he spotted his father—who was now assigned to first shift—and watched him work. He was in a field of tomatoes. Jacob watched him as he carefully passed from plant to plant. At each one he stopped and groped among the leaves, testing each round fruit for the tenderness that revealed its ripeness. Jacob observed that he selected only the brilliant red ones, leaving the green ones on the vine. Sometimes he selected an orange one, other times he didn't, and Jacob wondered what that meant. He also watched his father stop from time to time and quickly stuff a smaller one in his mouth, chew rapidly, and swallow before moving on. Jacob thought about his father's words the night before. Everyone got their fair share, he had said. After the third time his father ate a tomato, Jacob had to leave. But it wasn't only his father who was cheating—virtually all the workers could be seen popping fruits and vegetables into their mouths from time to time, always when no one else was nearby.

Seeing the workers together in the field, each oblivious to the others' illicit pickings, made him bitter. As with yesterday's theft, his sight made him a guilty witness, complicit in crimes that weren't his own. Today would be different, though. Today he would take no food. He wouldn't be like his father and the others. He remembered what Delaney had told him about her father the day before her death. *There's a lot about him you don't know*, she had said. From what he'd seen so far, this seemed to be true of everybody.

Jacob moved deeper into the fields. The whole area was carefully sectioned into grids and lined with modified pathminders to assist the growers in their work. The cultivated sections of land were enormous, and he walked for some time before approaching the periphery. There crops of wheat and corn alternated, creating beautiful patterns of green and gold, all at the peak of harvest. Here the workers used machines to help them collect the crops. He paused near a field to watch. In each plot two workers stood at either end of a tall row of corn, while a harvesting machine hummed its way down the row. He was fascinated by the large steel device that gleamed in the sun, thumping away in a steady rhythm as it crawled forward. The long, heavy arms of the harvester pulled the stalks of corn, drawing them into its belly, where the ears were separated and dropped into a bin that followed behind. The remaining plant material was then chopped into another bin as cattle feed. When the machine reached the end of a row, the worker removed its bins, dumped their contents into wagons, and replaced them. The machine automatically aligned itself at the next row and headed back to where the other worker waited to repeat the procedure.

He watched the harvester thread its way back and forth, leaving behind empty land dotted only by the stubble of cornstalks. Several pairs of large birds with bright red and blue feathers and broad, wedge-shaped beaks flew down and settled in the stubbled patch of field. They passed along the freshly cultivated earth, picking the ground for leftover kernels. He sat near them and lost himself in the crop gathering, relishing the aroma of freshly cut vegetation and the hypnotic hum of the harvester.

The machine moved to the end of the row closest to where Jacob sat. Before the grower had finished replacing a bin, the machine lurched rapidly, swinging itself in a ninety-degree arc. One of its arms swung as well, catching the confused worker in the side of the head. The man dropped to the ground instantly, not moving even when one of his legs came under the harvester as it shifted to the next row. It continued toward the other grower, spraying chopped cornstalks on the ground in the absence of the missing bin.

Jacob's heart pounded as he looked from the machine—slowly making its way down the row—back to the fallen worker. He had to do something. The man's partner stood at the far end of the field, oblivious to what had just occurred. It would be ten minutes before he had any idea that something was wrong. Who knew how much longer it would take to discover the accident; by then, it could be too late. Jacob sprang up and sprinted to the injured grower. He knelt down next to the man, feeling helpless, shocked by the bright red blood that flowed from the corners of the man's mouth. The man lay unconscious, and already a vicious purple bruise was forming along the right side of his face. And then there was the leg. Unable to close his eyes, he glanced at the mangled foot crushed into the ground, blood soaking into the pant cuff around it.

Jacob's first impulse was to scream for help, to alert the partner or anyone else nearby to rush the man to the infirmary, but he checked himself. To yell would mean discovery. He would have to explain not only why he was out here, but how he had managed to discover the fallen worker. He racked his brain to find a way out for both of them. The man's breathing was shallow and he moaned softly, as if he were simply wrestling with a bad dream and nothing more. But it was Jacob who felt as if he were trapped in a nightmare, agonizing as every second passed. Then his eyes fixed on the polished sounder pinned to the man's chest, and a solution appeared. He remembered learning that every sounder contained a panic function for use in emergencies. Jacob pounded the sounder three times in quick succession. Immediately a high pulsing tone rose and fell in a rapid beat. The piercing noise, which would last only a few minutes before draining the battery, stabbed into Jacob's ears, and he retreated. The pathminders closest to them began to wail in response, and the pitch of alarm transcended everything, even the sound of the harvester.

Jacob searched the far end of the row. The other grower emerged, paused, and began moving down the line, tracing along the edge of the corn with his left hand. As the man reached the harvester, he leaned over and, after a second of groping, flipped a switch. The engine died; the arms froze in midair and its spiked wheels stopped turning. The wailing calls seemed louder without the engine running. *Hurry, hurry!* Jacob thought, resisting the urge to scream out loud as the grower continued toward Jacob and the injured man, moving into a trot. Looking around, Jacob could see other workers coming toward him on the paths as well, emerging from the other fields with concern and curiosity on their faces. He realized he was about to be surrounded and ran to where he had been watching before, turning to see men and women gather around their fallen comrade. They carefully placed him in an empty wagon and began running the cart toward the settlement.

Looking down, Jacob saw wet blood on his hands. Feeling shaky and weak, he ran to catch up with the wagon and followed it to the infirmary, which was fortunately in the southern tier, close to the fields. For a half hour he sat like a statue on a bench outside the infirmary door, hoping to hear some news about the injured worker, but no one came out after the initial group of growers returned to the fields. After a while, having heard nothing and wanting to prevent suspicion by asking, he returned home.

It was only on the way home that Jacob realized he was walking into trouble. He opened the front door and, standing on the threshold, recognized the shape of his mother in the shadows. She was waiting. She knew that he had skipped school; the only question was what she had done about it and what she would do now. He debated whether to ignore her and head directly to his room or remain and call her name, as if he were unaware of her presence. Before he could decide, she spoke.

"Did you have a good day, Jacob?" she asked.

Jacob didn't want to lie, but he couldn't tell her. "It was fine," he mumbled.

"Aren't you going to ask me about my day?" she asked. Her voice was hollow and hoarse.

*Here we go,* Jacob thought. He could tell from the forced neutrality of her voice what was coming. "How was your day?" he asked.

"Wonderful. For the second time in two weeks I've had to lie for my son." Jacob inwardly breathed a sigh of relief. She had covered for him. "Care to tell me where you were?"

"I wasn't feeling good," he stated. "I needed to get some fresh air, so I went out to the north field." It was only a half-truth, but it was the best he could muster.

"Fresh air? All day? Come on, Jacob, I know you can do better than that."

"I fell asleep," he answered. An image of blood flashed through his mind.

"Fell asleep," she echoed in disbelief.

"Is that all?" he asked, wanting to leave.

"No, actually, it isn't. I've saved the best for last." Her voice sounded strangled now, as if someone else were speaking through her. Jacob's pulse quickened. What could it be? Did she know? How could she? "I was talking to some of the neighbors this morning," she said. "There's a rumor going around that there was a theft yesterday. Somebody broke into the storehouse and stole some food while everyone was at the Gathering."

"Really?" he said. He saw the hunched shape slipping through the streets in his mind's eye. He saw the dropped package in his hands. Suddenly her words coalesced and he realized what was about to happen.

"And behold," she continued, ignoring his response, "what do I find in my son's room this morning, but this"—an empty can bounced noisily on the ground before him—"and this"—another can. "There's more where this came from. Would you care to check?"

"No," he whispered.

"How could you?" she demanded with dismay.

"I'm not a thief," he said. He had to tell her. The theft, the accident . . . everything. He wasn't a thief; he wasn't bad. He had saved a man's life, and he could bring a thief to justice. Weren't those good things? Wouldn't they be enough to offset the sin of the vision that had brought these things about? She would have to accept him, no matter her belief, no matter what they both had always been taught.

Before he could tell her, she broke in. "What hurts, Jacob, is that you don't even seem to care about how this affects me. I know how much Delaney's death disturbed you, but it's been twice as devastating for me. She was my student. We worked together every day. She was like a daughter." She was crying now. "And now this. I don't know whether to believe you or not. You go off every day. Spend hours alone. Egan came by today to check on you. He said he's barely heard from you the last few days, that you've been keeping to yourself. This antisocial behavior, it's not like you. You never used to lie."

He didn't say a word. He was tempted to shout, *What about you?* and point out her hypocrisy. She had lied to the authorities twice. True, her lies had saved him, but all the more reason to be ashamed—they had all been taught that Harmony came first, that truth came first. Family came second. Maybe that was a lie; maybe in reality, truth didn't come first. Maybe the bonds of family were too difficult to break. He would never reveal those thoughts to her, though. He would appear ungrateful. Besides, she was right in a way—it had never truly occurred to him how difficult Delaney's death must've been, and must still be, for his mother. He couldn't tell her about his vision now; it would only make matters worse. She would lose another child. Better that she suspected him a thief, a loner. At least those things weren't permanent. They could be rationalized as simply a phase, the angst of a thirteen-year-old. He had had a chance to help Delaney and hadn't said the right thing; the only chance to help his mother now was to say nothing at all.

"All I know, Jake," she said, her voice groping for strength, reaching out through the darkness before his eyes, "is that this is the last time. I will never lie for you again. The next time something like this happens, you will have to leave our house and go to the fixers."

Jacob gasped. The fixers took in people who were having trouble with life in Harmony. Sometimes it was because they couldn't follow the rules; others went because they suffered from depression or anxiety. The fixers lived with them in seclusion, worked with them, and counseled them daily until they were cured and ready to resume life in the community. It was usually the last resort, and the people who were cured never acted quite the same after release. Jacob met one once when he was young. A woman in their tier had spent a year with the fixers, though he never found out why. Before she left, Jacob remembered her as loud and chatty. He remembered she would often corner his mother in the street and gossip or complain. He was too young to really know what she was talking about, but he remained fascinated by this bold and animated woman. Upon finally returning, she rarely spoke, and when she did, her words were slow and strangely muted. She died a few years later.

"I'll be good, Ma," he said softly, and went to his room.


Shortly afterward, Jacob heard his father come home. He opened the bedroom door and eavesdropped on his parents' conversation.

"It was pretty bad," his father said. "Thank God they got him to the infirmary in time."

"Is Mitchell going to be okay?" his mother asked.

"He lost a lot of blood, got a nasty concussion. Worst of all, the ghostbox had to amputate his foot, but he'll live." He paused. "It's strange, though. His sounder alerted everyone so quickly. But when they got there, he was unconscious. Nobody can figure out how he activated it."

"Maybe it went off on its own."

"They just don't do that, Gina. They should, but they don't."

"Maybe he activated it before passing out."

"Maybe. But when he came to, he couldn't remember doing it. The last thing he remembers is replacing the chopping bin. That's it."

"Well, he probably can't remember because of the concussion. Besides, who cares, Richard? He's alive, isn't he?"

"I guess. Talk about lucky; it could have been worse—he could have bled to death in the field before anyone noticed, or been dragged by that thing, or even sucked up into it—"

"Okay, I get it," his mother interrupted.

Jacob could hear his father's voice sharpen. "It pisses me off. This is the third time one of those pieces of garbage has malfunctioned this month. I warned Norris that someone was going to get hurt."

"No point getting upset. They'll get some new

harvesters eventually."

"Right," he said sarcastically. "Where's Jake? It's almost time for dinner."

"He's in his room" was all she said. Her voice revealed none of the anger Jacob knew was there. "Why don't *you* get him."

Jacob heard the heavy steps coming down the hall toward his room. He quietly closed the door and waited for his father, breathing a sigh of relief. The injured man would live.

Dinner was a silent affair, in itself not unusual, but in the stifling darkness of the house it seemed more strained than usual to Jacob. He could sense his mother's anger in every grating of the knife and fork against her plate, a cold anger that set him on edge. His father soon gave up making small talk but didn't seem to notice anything was amiss between wife and son. Jacob figured he was probably too tired to care after the long day of harvest. The image of his father gulping down tomatoes on the sly rose up in his mind as he listened to the man grunt and chew. He didn't seem any less hungry than usual. Then again, his father was always hungry.

"I can help do dishes, Ma," Jacob offered after dinner. "Don't bother," she snapped. He backed off, not wanting to rekindle her earlier rage.

He went to his room and lay back on the bed. He wasn't tired, but he didn't dare go back out to where his mother and father now sat listening to a Foundation broadcast. Still, just sitting in the blackness of his room had no appeal. He wished he could do something to ease the boredom or, better yet, make things right with his mother.

Suddenly he had an idea. Maybe he could do something to make up for all the pain he'd caused her lately. He got up and went out to the living room.

"I've got to go over to Egan's," he told his parents.

"Why?" his father asked.

"I told him I'd help him study for a test tomorrow. We're having final tests in school."

"You didn't mention it earlier," his father said.

"I forgot."

"I guess it's still early. I don't know, Gina, what do you think?"

"I don't care. He can do whatever he wants. He's good at that these days, isn't that right, Jacob?"

There was an awkward silence for a moment as Jacob hesitated, not wanting to engage her. Finally his father broke in.

"Go ahead, then. Just don't stay too late."

"It won't take long," Jacob replied, heading out. He

could already hear an argument starting as he closed the door behind him.

He knocked for the second time, but still there was no response. *Come on*, he thought. *He has to be home.* Jacob knocked a third time, louder now, but still all was quiet. He turned away from the high councilor's door and looked out. The sun had nearly reached the horizon, and the shadows in the street below were long. A pair of wind chimes rang faintly from a neighboring house in the evening breeze. With a sigh, he started down the ramp. All the way over he had been brimming with excitement at the idea of the gift, but now it looked like it would have to wait.

A sudden tone behind him stopped him and he turned back toward the door.

"Who is it?" the high councilor's voice said, sounding tinny and faint through the small speaker by the door, not at all the normal commanding boom Jacob was used to. Intercoms were installed in most of the common buildings, but few residences had them. Egan's house had one, but it had long since stopped working.

"It's me. Jacob Manford."

"Jacob?" The man sounded puzzled.

"I needed to ask you something," he replied. Jacob

began to worry that he'd disturbed him from something important.

"Yes. Come in."

Jacob opened the door and stepped into the hallway. A familiar smell flooded his senses as he entered. Delaney's scent still lingered in the house, and for a second he half expected to see her waltz into view. Here, though, his memory failed him; he realized he had no idea what she looked like. The impression faded as a figure appeared. Although the door was half open, the light outside was dim enough now that he could barely see. The high councilor was nothing more than a tall, dark shape enveloped in shadow at the opposite end of the hall.

"This is an unexpected pleasure, Jacob," the high councilor purred. "To what do I owe the honor?"

Jacob paused for a moment, gathering his courage. "I have a favor to ask. I know that when people die, their sounder is given away. I was just wondering if"— he hesitated—"maybe I could have Delaney's. To give to my mother," he added.

There was a long pause. As each second passed, Jacob's heart began to pound. Had he insulted the man? When the high councilor finally replied, his voice sounded strange, higher in pitch, tentative.

"That's a kind gesture, Jacob," he said, clearing his

throat. "Unfortunately, even if I wanted to, I couldn't let you have it, as I don't have it myself."

Jacob's heart sank at the man's words. "Who did you give it to?" he blurted out, too disappointed to realize the temerity of questioning Harmony's leader.

Again there was a pause. "I buried it with her."

"Oh," Jacob said, puzzled. He had never heard of that before.

"It was too painful for me to keep," the man added quickly. "I felt that the memory of its sound would be too much of a burden. As leader of the community, I carry enough burdens already."

"Oh," Jacob said again, trying to sort out the high councilor's words.

"I fault myself, now, for not having thought of giving it to Regina. She certainly would deserve it. But it is buried with the girl and there it will remain," he said, then added, as if to change the subject, "Your mother really misses her, doesn't she?"

"Yes," Jacob replied.

"And you too, I'm sure."

"Yes."

"Come here, Jacob," the high councilor commanded. Jacob stepped into the shadows until he felt the man's hand on his shoulder "I know this has been a struggle, young man, but as time passes you will learn to accept what happened. Acceptance is perhaps the greatest virtue. It is what our Truesight is based on. I know it seems heartless to say, but Delaney's death has no meaning in the larger scheme of things. One person, even myself, has no meaning other than that he or she is part of the larger whole, the community. Our community. Do you understand that?"

"Yes," Jacob replied faintly, feeling the firm grip on his shoulder.

"Of course you do. You're a smart young man. Everyone says so. Besides," he said, "Delaney is much better off now. She has gone deep into the darkness, far beyond the reaches of even our own meager attempts. She understands Truesight in a way that neither of us fully can until the day we join her. In life she struggled with it, as I think both you and I know, but in the end she embraced it. I am so proud of her."

Jacob didn't know what to say. He had struggled to accept that Delaney was gone, and felt that he had nearly done it, but somehow the high councilor's words chilled him. If what the man said was true, then Jacob's time in the light was only pushing him farther away from Delaney. But if anything, he now realized, his vision only made him feel closer to her, to what she had struggled with in life. He remembered again what she had confessed to her father the last time he had come into this house. Detaching himself from the councilor's grip, he turned back toward the door.

"Jacob," the high councilor said, and Jacob paused. "You need to help your mother understand this also. If your father cannot, you must. She'll come around. Your mother is a very special woman, very special. I feel fortunate that Delaney was able to have her in her life. We all are."

"Thanks," Jacob said. "I know."

He hurried from the house and ran home through the empty streets. He had come with high hopes and left feeling disappointed and confused. By the time he got home, the sun had long since set, there were no moons yet in the sky, and darkness had settled over the land.

# CHAPTER TWELVE

The next day Jacob went to school. All morning he had been having trouble concentrating, and now, sitting in orienteering class, he felt agitated and barely listened as Mr. Robison lectured. It wasn't just the conversation last night with Delaney's father that bothered him. Neither he nor his mother had spoken to each other during breakfast, and Jacob hoped her silence meant her anger was dissipating. However, it could also mean that it was still there, building beneath the surface, intensifying. He recalled the birthday picnic on the hill a few nights ago; in his mind he saw once again the coldness in her face. Then it had been directed toward his father. Had she been wearing the same face this morning toward him? He hadn't been able to tell in the dark.

All Jacob knew was that the more he saw of people's behavior, the less he understood. The last few days had been both exhilarating and bewildering. Last night, as he lay in bed, he began thinking about how his vision might impact his life permanently. It had been less than three weeks since his sight had slowly surfaced, and it was only the fourth day since he had begun seeing clearly. In that time so much had happened. He felt like he was being swung around, faster and faster, through a cycle of ecstasy and guilt, a circle that went nowhere. Would it always be this way? The prospect seemed exhausting.

"Is everyone ready?" Mr. Robison asked. Jacob pushed the thoughts of this morning aside and joined the class as they answered yes. "Okay, let's head outside."

They left the building and entered the school yard. Jacob blinked at the brightness, shielding his eyes from the sun. The students gathered near the mellow tone of the teacher's sounder. Mr. Robison tapped the pin on his chest and it went silent.

"Last week you were tested with the finders. Everyone did well, as they should—finders are easy to use. Today, however, you're going to be tested on finding someone without the help of a device. You've been playing seeker for fun ever since you were little. This time, it's for a grade."

Jacob looked at his classmates. Aside from Egan, he

didn't know who belonged to which face; he had been away from school two of the last three days and had been indoors nearly the entire time he was there. They all stared blankly forward, heads turned in the teacher's direction.

"Remember the sweeping techniques you've learned. Use your sounders and your knowledge of Harmony to assist you. As I mentioned earlier, the class will be divided into two groups. Each person will be matched with someone from the other group and will be required to find him or her as quickly as possible. I'll assign a specific place to each hider. Seekers, you'll be told only which tier your partner is in—after that, you're on your own. When you find your partner, return here, and when everyone is finished, we'll rotate so that the hiders become the seekers. Hiders, when you reach your assigned spot, wait in the open—no hiding behind bushes or buildings or in doorways. Right, Egan?"

"I wouldn't dream of it!" Egan said, and the students giggled.

Mr. Robison divided the class into two groups and assigned partners. Jacob was paired with Parker, a boy from the South Tier. He didn't know Parker well, but he had always gotten along with him. Parker's dark eyes pointed straight at Jacob. Jacob found the blank gaze disquieting. He felt vulnerable, though he knew the boy's eyes saw nothing. *It should be the other way around*, he thought. *He's the vulnerable one.* He fought the desire to look away and forced himself to return the stare, to absorb every feature of this person he had barely known over the years. The boy was taller than Jacob, with a dark complexion that matched his eyes. His black hair was longer than most of the others', falling down over his forehead and almost covering his eyes. Parker was quiet by nature. When he did speak, he did so slowly and thoughtfully. Like Jacob's mother, Parker's father was a musician. Jacob wondered why he had never tried to befriend the boy. After all, he had much more in common with him than Egan.

Mr. Robison walked down the row of hiders, assigning each to a spot in one of the four tiers. Before they left, the hiders briefly activated their sounders to remind the seekers of their identity. Parker was last in line. Jacob watched Mr. Robison lean down and whisper instructions in his ear. Parker nodded his head and moved away. Jacob's eyes followed him as he exited the school yard and headed toward the southern tier, eventually disappearing around the corner. Mr. Robison waited so the hiders would have enough time to reach their spots. While they were waiting, he told each of the seekers which tier to search in and reviewed their instructions.

"Remember, you'll be timed. When you hear your partner's sounder, move in and tap it silent. Then the two of you can come back here."

The seekers were finally cleared to leave, and one at a time they headed out in the same order in which their partners had left. Like Parker, Jacob was last. Leaving the school yard, he headed toward the South Tier. He considered closing his eyes; it would probably be fairer to the others. But whenever he tried, it felt too uncomfortable to move so blindly through the imposed darkness. Eventually he surrendered and kept his eyes open. The streets were quiet, as they usually were this time of day, but Jacob still observed people from time to time moving about their business. Weaving around them, he searched the eastern part, quickly moving down the main avenues between the hills, looking left and right into the side streets, where the houses lay. He saw no sign of Parker, so he headed to the western section.

On his way there, he stopped after rounding a corner. A girl stood in the middle of the street, her arms at her sides. He recognized her from his class; she had been one of the first to be sent away, and he had caught only a brief glimpse before she left. Now she stood alone, waiting to be found. Jacob moved closer, taking slow, quiet steps. He studied her face as he approached.

She had black hair, loosely tied back, that fell in curls around her face and onto her neck and shoulders. Thin, arched eyebrows seemed to pull up the corners of her eyes, giving her a regal, almost feline appearance. Jacob was transfixed. He could feel his heart pound as he moved closer. He noticed how her robe gathered tightly at her waist and how she stood so still with a patient look, her lips moist and slightly parted, forming a slight smile in repose. She was beautiful.

Jacob tried to be quiet. He was fifteen feet away and moving, but she hadn't seemed to notice him. He felt as if he were being drawn in to the girl, closer and closer, by an invisible cord. He paused only when a breeze suddenly arose and wafted her scent toward him. Lilacs. It was Beth, the girl he had been sent out into the hall to locate with the finder that day in school. He thought about that day, remembering the touch of her soft hand, warm but not sweaty. He wanted to touch her now, to confirm that it was really Beth, that she was really alive and not some statue or vision. He reached out his hand as he continued toward her, breathing quickly. A chord began to ring as their sounders moved within range. Both of them jumped back a step, startled, and the chord ceased. Jacob watched her as a look of confusion and perhaps fear disturbed the calmness of her face. She froze, listening for any noise.

"Susan?" she said.

Susan must be her partner. What should he say? He almost ran without uttering a word, but somehow it felt wrong not to say something.

"It's me—Jacob. Is that you, Beth?"

"Jacob!" she said, and the concerned look vanished. "Yes, it's me. You had me scared for a minute there; I didn't hear you approach."

"I can be pretty invisible when I want to be," he joked, and she laughed.

"Who are you searching for?" she asked.

"Parker. He's around here somewhere." He felt like an idiot. He should say something else, something clever, as Egan would, but he could only stare at the high cheekbones that were now flushed a light crimson. "Well, I better go" was all that came out.

"Good luck," she said. She was smiling; the corners of her mouth seemed to dance. Then, as Jacob moved forward to go around her, she moved too, going in his direction. He didn't prevent the collision, but reached his hands forward as they gently bumped, and steadied her. He pulled his hands away quickly, as if he were touching a plate from the oven. They exchanged mumbled apologies and he left her standing there. As he walked away he could feel the blood pumping through his entire body, and he felt mildly light-headed. He broke into a run, slowing only when he encountered someone briefly in the street, and moved rapidly through the section. He soon found Parker. The boy was sitting outside the infirmary, right where Jacob had sat yesterday. He approached Parker and tapped his pin, and the two of them headed to the school yard.

"That was fast," Parker commented. "I feel like I barely got there before you showed up."

Jacob didn't reply, and for the rest of the way back neither of them spoke. When they entered the school yard, Mr. Robison was amazed.

"Jacob! My God, this is a record," the teacher said. "How did you do it?"

"I was lucky, I guess" was all Jacob said.

It took more than half an hour before everyone was finally back. When they had gathered, Mr. Robison praised Jacob in front of everyone, and they applauded. Suddenly he felt ashamed. He didn't deserve any of it and wished he had waited longer before finding Parker or, better yet, had closed his eyes and searched for his partner the way he was supposed to.

Mr. Robison divided them again. This time it was Jacob's turn to hide. He stood in line, waiting for his teacher's instructions, and stared at Beth in the row across from him. He watched her as she talked quietly with the girl next to her. He wondered what Beth was saying to her friend. Maybe she was talking about him. A hand shook his shoulder, and he started.

"Hello, Jacob. Wake up." It was Mr. Robison.

"What?" he answered confusedly. He looked around. Everyone in his row had left for a hiding place. Only the students across from him remained.

"I don't know what to make of you these days, Jacob," the teacher remarked. "Either you're doing something amazing, or you act as if you're deaf as well as blind." The students giggled at the joke, all except Parker, who remained as placidly stoic as he had earlier.

"Sorry," Jacob muttered.

Mr. Robison bent over and cupped his hands around Jacob's ear.

"Auckland End," he whispered.

"Okay," Jacob said, and left the yard in the direction of his own North Tier. Auckland End was a cul-de-sac only a couple streets past his own. He paused at the fountain in his district's little square and splashed cool water on his face and neck. Looking around, he saw some flowers in a nearby bed. He was drawn to the yellow ones, each with more than a dozen thin petals around a black center. He picked five, breathing in their delicate scent. He decided he would pass his own street on his way to the assigned spot and stop at home. If he couldn't give her Delaney's sounder, then maybe the bouquet would placate his mother. He used to gather flowers for her all the time when he was younger, and she'd always loved it.

Jacob turned onto his street. He was at the door, reaching for the handle, when suddenly he heard voices coming directly from the other side. Just as he began wondering what his father was doing home in the middle of his shift, he heard the latch begin to turn. He decided to play a joke and surprise them, and leaped to the side and crouched down behind the flowering shrub that grew beside the doorway, deactivating his sounder to avoid discovery. A man stepped into the light, followed by his mother, but it wasn't his father. Through the leaves Jacob caught a glimpse of the man's face before he turned around. He didn't recognize the man with eyes so pale they seemed almost white and a long, dark beard streaked with gray. The pair lingered in the doorway, facing each other. Jacob's eyes widened as he watched them embrace. They didn't speak, only kissed, their arms wrapped around each other, her hand on the back of his neck. Then they parted, and his mother went inside and closed the door, leaving Jacob frozen behind the bush.

It was a long time before Jacob moved. He was stunned by what he had just seen. For the second time that day his heart pounded and his stomach fluttered, but whereas he had felt exhilarated before, he now felt confused and sick. He threw the flowers aside and returned to the square. When Parker appeared, Jacob quietly moved to intercept him, and they headed back to the school. When the exercise was over and the students were released for the day, Jacob approached Egan.

"Can I stay at your house tonight?" he asked, trying not to sound desperate.

"Why?" Egan demanded, his face cold and neutral.

"Please, Egan. I just need to."

"I don't know," Egan said. "You've practically ignored me for the last three days. I was beginning to think you'd found another best friend."

"Of course not," Jacob said. "I've had a lot on my mind."

"Fine, come over if you want," Egan said before breaking into a smile. "After all, it would be an honor to have the king of seekers grace my humble abode." Egan laughed. Jacob tried to laugh too, but the teasing compliment rekindled the feeling of shame.

When he got to Egan's house, Jacob called his mother and told her where he was. It felt strange talking to her—he couldn't get the image of the kiss out of his mind—and he hung up as quickly as possible. That night, he hardly slept. When he did manage to drift off, he had horrible dreams. Images of the last few days rose up and blended together. Beth, his mother and her lover, the blood-soaked grower, the thieving neighbor—all of them seemed to form some insidious drama against him. He fled, struggling into a distorted landscape in which the moon kept rising over and over again, pulling the grass up into the sky until it collapsed and smothered him with a blanket of darkness.

As Jacob awoke, the smothering sensation lingered with him in the utter blackness of the subterranean house. It was morning, but everyone still slept; he could hear Egan nearby, his slow breathing rhythmic and relaxed. Jacob rose silently and left without saying good-bye. The morning surrounded him with sharpness and detail; every leaf, every door, every stone in the street, was perfect in its clarity. Everything was perfect—everything except people like his mother, his father, his neighbors, the workers, and himself. *We are all deceiving one another*, he thought, looking down. His long shadow preceded him as he walked in the early-morning sun. *I am the greatest deceiver of all.* He could stand it no longer. He knew he had to tell someone his secret.

# CHAPTER THIRTEEN

The next day Jacob decided to reveal his secret to Egan. He felt he should probably tell his parents, but he just couldn't do it. These days his father was busy with the harvest, laboring long hours in the fields and storehouses, and when he was home, he was so irritable from exhaustion that Jacob stayed out of his way, as he always did each year during harvest. Besides, he had never been close with his father, at least when it came to talking about real things. As for his mother, he had been avoiding her as much as possible these last two days since seeing her with the other man. When they were together, they barely spoke.

It wasn't the illegality of his mother's behavior that really bothered him. Adultery was strictly forbidden, but rarely was anyone accused of it. Before these past few weeks Jacob would have believed that meant it never happened, but now he wasn't sure. Maybe it happened a lot; after all, most of the marriages in Harmony were arranged by the council and representatives of the Foundation. The more he witnessed, the more he realized that people probably broke the rules all the time. If so, then what good were the rules? Why bother to pay lip service to principles and then do the opposite? Jacob couldn't figure it out. *Maybe that's the way it's supposed to be,* he thought. Maybe it was better to have rules, even if people failed to obey them, than to have none at all. Maybe it was better for people to do so and feel civilized, even if they weren't, than to give in to any impulse freely without guilt.

Besides, wasn't he a walking, talking, *seeing* violation of the most sacred tenet of Harmony and its Foundation? He was as bad as any of them, worse than any of them, including his mother. No, it didn't bother him that she had committed a significant crime; it was more visceral than that. It was the image in his mind of the caress, of the kiss he had witnessed, that repulsed him every time it surfaced in his memory. Maybe it was the betrayal, but the betrayal was more against his father than him. All he knew was that it filled him with a cold anger, just like the look he had seen on his mother's face the night of his birthday. He probably bore that look now. How long had the affair been going on? A week? A month? A year or more? Maybe his father was aware, but it seemed unlikely. That left it to Jacob to tell. But he realized he never could. Instead, he had another secret to tell, a far more ominous one that trivialized all the darker things he had seen.

Someone had to be told. And so it fell to Egan. They had shared secrets before, about the small things they felt or did, and Egan had never told anyone the thoughts that Jacob shared. He could count on him now to do the same—even with a secret like this one. He needed to unburden himself before things got out of control, and because he didn't trust himself, he would have to trust somebody else, an ally who could help him sort everything out. Egan sometimes lacked gravity and sincerity, but he also possessed a boldness, a clarity that Jacob felt he himself lacked, no matter how clearly he saw the world. For Egan, life was simple and defined.

The two of them were in the main square, returning home from school—the next to the last day—having paused near the north exit, where they usually parted. Jacob would head north and Egan would go east. The square was almost empty as Jacob looked beyond Egan and surveyed the area. The afternoon sun was cooler now and cast shadows along the western edge, leaving that part of the square bathed in blue. A few old men occupied benches in the shadows, lined up as if waiting for something to come take them someplace else. They hardly spoke; they sat silently, blind eyes pointed straight ahead, moving only to brush the flies away. Whatever they were saying, Jacob couldn't hear; as always, soft music played over the speakers that lined the square, the same speakers that projected the voice of the high councilor at each Gathering. Bouncing off the emptiness of the open space, the music sounded hollow and lonely, as if it sensed nobody listened.

Jacob and Egan were discussing school, anticipating their last day tomorrow, wondering how things would change. Over and over Jacob tried to say the words that kept rising to his mouth like dry heaves. He felt detached, pushed out of himself, watching from the outside as this stranger refused to tell his secret. Now Egan was telling him about his specialization, about the news his father had told him last night. None of them were supposed to find out until after the harvest, when the work was done, but his father had told him; they shared secrets too. Egan would be leaving, going on a starship to Earth, back to the Foundation with his father and mother to be trained—for what, he didn't really know.

As they stood side by side facing the edge of the square, Egan quietly revealing the news, Jacob stared straight ahead at the wall. Like many of the buildings in Harmony, it was covered with burnished steel sheets that mirrored a warped reflection. He looked at the two of them standing together, his friend not as tall but standing squarely, while he slouched next to him. He couldn't see either of their faces; the mirroring sheets blurred their features, reminding him of his foggy sight before the clarity. He realized that he had never seen his own face. What did he look like?

"Maybe it won't be so bad," Egan was saying. "Besides, I'm sure I'll be back. I'll probably be a councilor someday, like my father. At least that's what he says. Maybe you will too. You're smart. Smarter than I am, probably. I asked my father about your specialization, but he wouldn't tell me. Still, I'm sure it'll be something good. What do you think?"

"I don't know," Jacob replied. He wasn't even sure he cared anymore. Just a few weeks ago it had been all he could think about, a source of subtle but constant anxiety. Now it seemed a trivial concern.

"Oh!" Egan burst out, startling Jacob. "I almost forgot." He dug into his pocket and produced a small black box. He reached out and took Jacob's arm, placing the box in his hand. It was a finder.

"Where did you get this?" Jacob asked.

"I took it from school, stupid. I figured we could have at least one last adventure before I leave."

"Why are you giving it to me?" Jacob asked, tucking it away in his bag. The whole thing irritated him. He needed to tell Egan now before he lost every bit of courage, and this was a distraction.

"You know my father. Mr. Suspicious. If he caught me with it, he'd kill me. You don't mind hanging on to it for me, do you? After all, you've said yourself that your parents—"

"Egan, I can see," he said. There—it was out. For a moment the world stopped. Even the music ceased briefly as one song ended and another began. Jacob watched Egan's reflection as the figure shifted uncomfortably.

"Yeah . . . right. Anyway, I know we can have some fun with this before anyone notices it's missing. So hang on to it, just for tonight. And whatever you do, don't tell anyone," Egan said.

"I can see," Jacob said again, so quietly this time that even he had trouble hearing himself above the music that wheedled in the background.

"Yeah, Jacob. You said that before," Egan replied, practically shouting in contrast. "I don't get it. What are you saying?"

"I'm saying," Jacob hissed, pulling his friend closer, "that I can see. Literally, with my eyes." He scanned the area nervously. No one was nearby. The square was vacant except for the old men and three women who had just entered from the southern tier. He stared at Egan, who now faced him. His brow was crinkled and a slight frown formed along his pressed lips. Suddenly his eyebrows reversed themselves into an arch, and the lips curled back to reveal his teeth.

"I get it!" Egan said. He tilted back his head and laughed. His howls bounced around the square like an echo and seemed to drown out the music. The sound terrified Jacob; he wanted to cover the laughing mouth with his hands, anything to quiet the reverberating noise. The women halted at the echoes, and the old men suddenly cocked their heads in unison. Finally Egan stopped laughing enough to speak through gasping breaths. "Jacob, you never cease to amaze me. I realize I've made plenty of off-color comments and bad jokes, but I've never heard anything so obscene, and with such perfect timing. Bravo!" he said, and briskly applauded.

*This is it*, Jacob thought. *All I have to do is go along, and it'll be as if I never said anything.* He was tempted for a second to recover himself, to admit to the tasteless comment, but he suddenly didn't want to. He was an obscenity, sight and all. Why not admit it?

"I'm serious," Jacob said quietly, so no one else could possibly hear. "I can see. Totally. Clearly. I can see you right now." And he could; he could see the look of shock and horror creeping over his friend's face, deeper with every word he spoke. Egan stepped backward, away from him and toward the wall, touching it, as if desperate for something solid in order to orient himself.

"I don't understand," Egan finally said. "How did this happen? . . . For how long?" he stammered.

"I don't know how, but it happened. It started only a couple weeks ago. At first it was just a light, and then blurry shapes and hazy colors. Last week I started seeing clearly. The race—in the north field, remember?"

Egan nodded. "Your birthday," he said. "And you've been able to see since then? You've been walking among us, staring at us, at me, the entire time? So that's how you did so well on the test the other day."

"That's not important. Egan, I don't know what to do." Jacob watched as Egan took another step backward. The expression remained on his friend's face, the look he had never expected to see. This wasn't going well. "It just happened," he said pleadingly.

"I can't imagine. What's it like?" Egan asked. Jacob could hear the wavering in his voice. The look of horror was fading. In its place, Jacob could see anguish and confusion. Anything was better than fear. If Egan was afraid, what did that mean for him?

"I don't know how to explain it," he said. "It's as if everything about yourself is suddenly bigger and smaller at the same time. The whole world is bigger because you can see the distances. You can see the sky and watch the grass move and people walk. The sun rises and sets, and the moon climbs too, across your eyes. And all the time the outside edge is pushed farther back, you're pushed farther in, growing less and less. You realize you're nothing in the midst of the world out there. When I was blind, I had only myself, no matter who or what was around me. Nothing distracted me from myself, not even the sounds that defined the space around me. I was inside. Now I'm still in there, but I'm surrounded by everything I've seen. Images emerge without my even thinking about them." He realized he'd closed his eyes while he was talking, trying to explain the inexplicable. Now, as he opened them, he saw that Egan had turned his back on him, was leaning against the wall.

"What are you going to do?" Egan asked in a strained whisper.

"I don't know," Jacob said, "but you can't tell anyone."

"I can't? Maybe not, but you should. Tell the council what you told me. They'll know what to do."

"I can't do that. What if they do something to me?"

"That's good, isn't it? They can fix you. It's not your fault."

"Why do we have to tell anyone? Just keep it between ourselves."

"Jacob, this isn't some prank, or even like sneaking out during a curfew. This is big—bigger than you or me. Anyway, people deserve to know you can see them, because otherwise . . . I don't know, it's creepy."

"Is that what I am? Creepy?" The words rushed from his mouth before he could think. "Let me tell you, Egan, you're creepy. You and everyone else. Your eyes are open but they see nothing. All around you people are doing things you don't know about, things you don't want to know about. You live in a small world. You live in a tiny place where you're taken care of. You look healthy, your cheeks are full, but most of the others don't look so good. Half of them are skin and bones. Their faces are thin. *That's* creepy, Egan. Not me." Jacob trembled as he spoke. He knew he shouldn't be saying these things, but he blurted them out regardless.

"Maybe I do live in a small world, but not for long. Soon I'll be far away on Earth, and you'll still be stuck here, watching everyone with your creepy eyesight, if you're lucky."

*Lucky? What does he mean by that?* Jacob wondered. He became scared.

"Egan, I'm sorry. I didn't mean what I said before," he apologized.

"Don't worry about it," Egan said, turning away to hide the tears welling up in his eyes. Jacob had never known his friend to cry before—except the few times he was hurt during a fall—and he didn't want to now.

"I'm only telling you my secret because you're my best friend and I can trust you."

"I know," Egan said, turning away again, this time to leave. "Hey, I have to go."

"Don't tell anyone," Jacob pleaded. "Promise me."

"I won't," Egan said, walking away, "I promise. We'll talk more tomorrow."

Jacob watched him leave. Then he was out of sight, and Jacob realized he was alone in the square. The women had left through the east or west exits, unaware of the boys' conversation; even the old men had disappeared—whatever they were waiting for must have come and gone. All that remained was himself and the music. A melodramatic march, some Foundation standard, was droning weakly through the speakers. As Jacob listened, the player began to skip, causing the same hysterical measure to repeat itself over and over and over. Nobody noticed to fix it.


They came for him the next day. It was the last day of school, and everyone was outside enjoying lunch in the sun. Several times that morning Jacob had tried to talk to Egan, but the opportunity for a private moment never arose. Egan had also failed to appear at their usual meeting place in the square before heading to school.

"I missed you this morning," Jacob said, approaching him before Mrs. Lawson's class.

"I woke up late. I barely made it here on time" was all Egan said. His voice sounded distant, and Jacob became nervous. It wasn't the fear of being discovered that gripped him initially, it was the fear of rejection. All last night he had chastised himself for revealing his secret to Egan, for telling anyone. He had become so accustomed to his sight in the short time since its arrival that it hadn't occurred to him just how outrageous the news might be to anyone. All their lives they had been taught to think of sight as an anathema. Of course Egan would react the way he did. Why hadn't Jacob thought of that ahead of time? Why would he think anyone would understand?

Still, he didn't believe that Egan would tell anyone else. But as soon as the two men appeared at the entrance of the school yard, calling several teachers over, Jacob knew that they had come for him. He watched as the men whispered to his teachers, who physically recoiled at the words spoken to them, the words of his secret. Mr. Robison was now approaching him where he sat among his classmates, eating a piece of bread and a tomato. Jacob stared down at the half-eaten fruit, at its cluster of seeds and the brilliance of its red skin, torn along the edges. He watched the other students, laughing and talking to one another. They were beautiful, the girls and the boys, and he did his best to savor these last few seconds when he was still one of them, another child content to live in darkness.

Coming to the edge of the group, Mr. Robison called to him. "Jacob, come here, please. The listeners want to speak to you."

Immediately all conversation halted. If the listeners wanted someone, it was never good. Jacob looked around him. The students now began whispering to one another, and he could hear the quiet questions buzzing like newly hatched flies. Only Egan, who sat nearby, said nothing; his head was bent, his hands covered his ears. Jacob rose and walked through the clusters of students on the grass to where Mr. Robison waited. He could see the struggle on the man's face, the attempt to be neutral, to hide the fear or repulsion that wanted to show itself. Whether he was trying to hide it from Jacob or himself, Jacob wasn't sure. Mr. Robison slowly offered his hand to lead Jacob away, as was the custom. His arm was trembling.

"That's okay, you don't have to bother," Jacob said. The teacher dropped his arm, and Jacob thought he saw relief on the man's face. They walked side by side to the street.

"You know why they're here, then?" Mr. Robison asked.

"Yes," Jacob answered.

"Is it true?"

"Yes."

"Don't be scared. Tell the truth. It'll be easier on everyone."

Jacob knew Mr. Robison was doing his best to be nice, but it only made him feel worse. He felt like a criminal, as if he had just killed someone. They reached the listeners, who stood composed and impassive. They were businesslike and spoke in an abrupt, formal manner that implied the weight of authority.

"Jacob, the council wishes to meet with you about your sight. We're escorting you there now," one of them said, an older man with gray hair shorn close.

"Will anyone else be there with him? What about his parents?" Mr. Robison asked.

"It's none of your concern," the other listener barked.

"I want to know," Jacob said.

"We spoke to them this morning. Your parents will

meet you at the council house."

"Come on, Maury," Mrs. Lawson said. "Let's get back to the students." She had been standing to the side when Jacob arrived. Now she stepped in and took Mr. Robison's arm to lead him away.

"She's right. Return to the children. We have everything under control here," the older man assured them.

*Under control?* Jacob thought. What did they think he might do?

"Good luck," Mr. Robison called behind him as he and Mrs. Lawson walked away. The students in the yard had finished eating and were now grouped together along the fence that separated the school yard from the street, straining to hear any part of the conversation. Jacob heard the teachers order them inside. He wondered what they would tell them.

The two men came over and stood on either side of him. Each one took a hand, keeping Jacob firmly between them.

"Don't try to run away," the younger listener warned.

"Why would I?" Jacob asked. He tried to sound calm, but he could hear the quaking in his voice.

"Do you realize your transgression? How serious it is?" the man asked.

"Lay off," the older man ordered. "He's just a kid."

"He's a Seer," the other sneered. Jacob closed his eyes; it was the first time he'd been called that.

"I guess you've heard," Jacob said.

"We hear everything," the younger listener replied with a grin.

# CHAPTER FOURTEEN

The council house wasn't far from the school. They journeyed in silence; the listeners remained mute the rest of the way, and Jacob wasn't particularly interested in talking to them, either. Instead he thought about what the council might ask him and what he would say. They passed quickly into the southern tier and up the rise to the council house, set into the hillside. It was one of the largest hills in Harmony. A wide entrance with double doors propped open on either side gaped from the earth. The opening that led into the hall was black, a giant mouth waiting to swallow and consume him. Walking up the straight road lined with pathminders, Jacob avoided looking at that dark hole. Instead he looked beyond where the elevation revealed the landscape to the south. He could see the fields, could make out the growers moving around the vast square patches of crops, dark little shapes scurrying to and fro.

Everyone was doing his job, oblivious to what was happening here on the hill.

A breeze picked up and the sound of wind chimes broke the silence. Jacob turned his head to discover they were standing before the entrance. Two large sets of chimes, each a cluster of silver pipes waving and singing, hung from the doors. Above the entrance a large striped cat lay stretched on top of the frame, staring down at him with yellow eyes. The eyes were beautiful the way they set upon him, locking themselves with his own gaze. They were different from the cow's eyes he'd seen earlier. Those alien eyes had taken him in and then left him, disinterested and dull. These eyes penetrated him, remained fixed and knowing, as if a moment of understanding and solidarity now passed between them, a secret shared.

*Don't worry. Don't be afraid*, they said. *You are not alone.*

*I feel like it*, he replied silently. *What do I tell them?* he asked, but the spell was broken as the cat severed its gaze and stared away with an indifferent flick of the tail.

"Come on," the older listener said, "it's time." They both tugged him from where he had paused.

As soon as he passed through the chamber doors, the darkness enveloped him. Coming from the bright sun into the cool chamber felt as if someone had suddenly placed a blindfold over his eyes. After a few seconds, however, the light filtering in from outside, faint as it was, brought out shapes before his adjusting eyes. He could see his parents off to the right, silent and still. He couldn't distinguish their faces and wondered what they were feeling right now.

"Hi, Ma. Hi, Dad," he said, trying not to sound scared.

"Hello, Jake," his father said quietly. His voice didn't sound angry, the way Jacob thought it might. His mother said nothing.

"Come here, Jacob," the familiar voice of the high councilor called out. Jacob walked farther into the hall and approached the council. They sat along the far end of the room, six figures in chairs against the wall. They were barely visible at this end of the chamber, and aside from the white folds of their gowns, which draped to the floor, he could only see their general shapes.

"We're sorry to have pulled you away from your last day of school, Jacob," the high councilor said, seated in the middle of the group, "but we didn't want to delay any further. We've already spoken to your parents. Unfortunately they were unable to be helpful, though I know they tried. It seems you've done a good job keeping this change a secret—until yesterday, that is."

"Did Egan tell on me?"

"Egan did what he was supposed to do," Egan's father, sitting next to the high councilor, broke in. "If it makes you feel any better, he clearly didn't want to tell me. However, I know my son. I know when something is bothering him. He was disturbed by your revelation yesterday, Jacob."

"So was I," Jacob countered.

"Of course you were, Jacob," the high councilor said. "You should know from the outset that you're not in trouble."

"Just tell us what happened," said a woman's voice on the far left of the shapes. He recognized it as Sonya Donato's. She lived the next street over from Jacob and his parents. "We can't help you if you don't help us."

Jacob wondered what that help would be. He said nothing at first. Fingers of light curled around his legs, casting shadows along the swirling stone of the floor tiles at his feet. For several moments the only sound was the muted tone of the chimes blowing softly from the doorway. Then even that stopped, and there was silence.

"Go on, Jacob. Tell them," his father urged from the corner.

Jacob finally told them. He recounted the last three weeks, about the headaches, the brightening, the colors, the blurry shapes, and the clarity. He left out some of the details, such as his neighbor's theft, and mentioned nothing about what he had witnessed that day his father was working in the fields, leaving his mother alone with the man he had seen outside his door. He was tempted to mention saving the grower's life, but he was certain they wouldn't want to hear it.

"What do you think of all this, Jacob? Do you like having sight?" the high councilor asked when Jacob finished his story.

Jacob wasn't sure what to say. "It's interesting. It makes things easier," he said finally.

"Easier is not always better, Jacob," another councilor said. "The challenges posed by our blindness strengthen us, make us a better people. Surely you know this from school."

"Jacob," the high councilor said, "long ago we abandoned the world of Seers because we understood that appearances can mislead. Vision corrupts the mind with its distractions."

Yes, of course. He had heard all these things many times at school and at the Gatherings. They had always made sense. Now, after everything, they still made sense in some ways, maybe even more so. He had certainly been distracted these past few weeks and had witnessed plenty of corruption, including his own dishonesty, but there was more to it than that.

"I've seen a lot of beautiful things," he said. "The plains, the moons, birds, flowers. Aren't those things important?"

"What is beauty, Jacob?" Egan's father said. "Isn't it all relative? Isn't there beauty in the songs your mother makes, and even those of the birds? The flower's scent is its true essence, what it is within. Those sights you've seen, those pictures that you find so pretty, are merely superficial."

"Beauty is beauty," Jacob replied. He didn't believe a word Mr. Spencer said, but he didn't know what else to say.

"If you'd never seen them, you wouldn't miss them," Mr. Spencer continued, ignoring him. "You know, Jacob, as one of the Oedipi, I used to see, back home on Earth. When I joined the Foundation, I relinquished my sight. It was the best thing I ever did. Of course those things you mention have a certain appeal to the average person, but I don't miss them. You don't realize how lucky you are to be raised in a community that is willing to penetrate deeper, to turn inward and have the courage to take what an ignorant person would find a weakness and make it their greatest strength."

"I'm sure these last few weeks have been terrible for you," the high councilor sympathized. "You never asked for any of this to happen. We feel nothing but sympathy for your ordeal."

"How *could* this have happened?" his father asked.

The high councilor answered, "There have been only a few other cases like this in the history of the colony. Once in a great while, a reversion in the genetic code of a fetus seems to occur. It usually manifests itself immediately at birth, when it can be corrected without surgery by covering the infant's eyes at the earliest stages of development. Deprived of visual stimulation, the neural pathways are soon dissolved. In general, the process is too tedious and unreliable to use on a regular basis, but it becomes an effective remedy in those rare situations."

Jacob remained silent. He didn't understand all of the high councilor's words, but the matter-of-fact way the man spoke about these matters chilled Jacob the same way it had when he'd spoken of his daughter a few days ago.

"What's unusual with Jacob's case is that it happened so late in life," Mrs. Donato said. "We've contacted the Foundation about the situation. Perhaps they'll have some information on how this could have happened. For now think of it simply as an oversight on nature's part. In the meantime we'll have to decide what to do with your son. Trust us to do what's best for Harmony."

The council asked no more questions and told Jacob and his parents to return home; a judgment would be forthcoming. As they were leaving, Jacob looked back at the council. They remained silent and unmoved.

"Remember, Jacob," the high councilor said, "justice is blind."

None of them spoke on the way home. Jacob wanted to say something to break the awkwardness of the moment, but the day's events hung over them, looming and oppressive. He walked behind his parents, watching the two of them as they reached out to each other and clasped hands. The intimacy of their touch, as surprising as it was, should have warmed him. Instead the sign of closeness made him feel more alone than ever. They turned the corner to their street. Jacob could see some of the neighbors standing or sitting on their doorsteps. Obviously the news had spread over the course of the afternoon. As his mother passed near a pathminder, the tone of her sounder called out. The lingerers quickly scuttled into their houses; the street echoed with the clap of closing doors. His parents flinched at the sound.

Jacob went to bed immediately after dinner. He

couldn't wait to steal away from his parents, who said little to him and seemed not to know how to deal with the change in their son. His father made small talk, mostly about work, and avoided anything that might touch on the day's events. Since the meeting at the council house, his mother had uttered few words. He wished she would scream at him, call him names, anything but give him the silent treatment, which in the total darkness of the house was depressing. She was like a ghost; he could feel her presence, but nothing more. He suspected she was probably considering his change. First Delaney, and now her own son. Before leaving the table, he moved tentatively to her chair. He touched her shoulder, the way he had the morning of his birthday when he left her to roam on his own.

"I'm sorry, Ma," he said.

She didn't answer but pulled him to her lap. She squeezed him hard, and he let her, shaking as her sobs racked her body. He wished he too could cry, but after today's events, he felt too numbed, too frightened, to give anything away. She held him as if he were a baby again, held him for a while, then let go.

Around eleven Jacob, unable to sleep, heard a knock at the front door. He maneuvered quickly to his bedroom door and opened it a crack. It was Mrs. Donato. He listened as she gave his parents the news.

"The council has decided that Jacob will be submitted to the ghostbox tomorrow for surgery to remove his eyesight."

"Is that necessary?" his mother asked. Fear sounded in her voice.

"Word's spread. The news of your son's difference has already created a significant disturbance among the people. Many are uncomfortable with the idea of living with a Seer in their midst. If Jacob is to remain in the colony, his sight must be corrected."

"It might as well be sooner than later," his father responded.

"We agree," the councilor said. "There's going to be a special midday Gathering tomorrow. Bring your son. And one more thing," she added before leaving, "we have decided that when the ghostbox operates, it will also be programmed to wipe Jacob's memory of the last few weeks. As far as your son is concerned, he'll never have seen a thing."

Jacob pretended to be asleep when his parents came in. They woke him up and told him the council's decision; they didn't speak of the memory wipe.

"Are you really going to let them do this to me?" he asked.

In the dark he could hear the awkwardness in his father's voice. "Jacob, we're not happy about the situation, but it's the council's order. We all have to do our best to go along."

"Think about your fellow citizens. You'll be setting a good example for the community," his mother assured him. "This wasn't meant to happen to you. In the end, you'll have lost nothing."

When they left, he lay there stunned. *Who are those people?* he asked himself. These strangers couldn't be his parents. Maybe his father could say those things, but certainly not his mother. She had come to his aid, covered for him several times—why not now? Maybe she was making good on her threat. She had warned him that she was finished helping him. These past few days, and especially today, he could sense the struggle within her, the detachment, the withdrawal; overwhelmed by the loss of one child, perhaps she had no other way to cope with what was happening to her son. Most likely, she and his father had no choice and were simply following orders. Where convenience and necessity met, what else could result but complicity?

Of course they had no choice. He had no choice. It was the will of Harmony—hadn't he always known that that's what set them apart? They didn't choose the selfishness of individual needs or wants. That was left to the Seers, who allowed themselves the indulgence of personal will and who suffered for it, living lives of chaos, each pursuing individual desires, oblivious to the good of others. He tried to relax in the darkness, to reconcile himself to the inevitable future of tomorrow. The councilors had inferred that his vision was an illness. Maybe he *was* sick. They were going to operate on him, after all. Didn't they do something like that only when someone was ill? Tomorrow the computer would make him well; the machine would repair the oversight, would correct nature's interference in the higher aims of humankind. And it would do more. It would ease the soul with forgetfulness, would take away those sights that had disturbed him and erase his crimes. He would be remade back into what he was—a boy who couldn't hurt anyone, who could again be a part of the community that had cared for him and raised him. He could be innocent again. It didn't matter whether he wanted it or not.

Fumbling in the dark, he picked up the new music box from his bureau. He hadn't played it once since his parents gave him the gift; the few times he'd tried, he found himself resisting. It didn't feel right somehow. It was no longer a part of him, and thinking about the song aroused a sadness in him that he had never felt before. The same thing happened now. His hand refused to open the lid, so instead he held it tightly, felt its weight in his palm, its textured metal surface and sharp corners.

*Most people would consider me lucky*, he thought. *Your life changes. You lose your innocence and it's gone forever; no choice there, either.* He tried telling himself this, but somehow it wasn't enough. There was that other voice there too, the one he had heard before, underneath and rising. It told him that he was different, not only from everyone else but also from himself. That person he once was, that he was sentenced to become again, had disappeared. It could never return, no matter what a computer did to him. Besides, even if he no longer remembered what he had become, everyone else would; he would always stand apart from them, never knowing why.

His mother had told him that in the end he'd have lost nothing. The voice warned him he would, in fact, lose everything. The images—the calm beauty of the skyline, the faces of his family and friends, even the bright blood of a wounded grower—would disappear, as would the freedom to move unhindered through the world, able to focus on richness beyond the self. Most of all, he would lose knowledge—of the inadequacies of human nature, of all the lies that penetrated Harmony like cracks in a foundation, of all the truths that his sight had shown him. All these things were now a part of who he was. In losing them, he would lose himself.

Memories of Delaney flooded his mind, leaving a hollow aching in their wake. He missed her now more than he ever had before. She would have understood him; she wouldn't have abandoned him like Egan, like his mother, like everybody else. He smiled grimly thinking back to all the cutting jokes and criticisms, the impersonations, even the sadder moments of alienation. Her words and deeds that had irritated him with their outrageousness no longer seemed beyond the pale. He understood her now, when it was too late. Most of all, he thought back to her desperate plea to her father the day before her death. *I want to see*, she had said. Jacob had received her wish instead. It had come to him unasked and changed him in ways he had never hoped for, yet wouldn't hope now to be without. It should have come to her. She would have had the strength to yield it. He yearned to be close to her now. Then it dawned on him. Maybe he could.

The house was quiet; his parents had gone to bed. Grabbing the finder Egan had asked him to hold on to, Jacob crept from his room and down the hall, then slipped outside. He headed toward the cemetery. He had never visited the burial grounds before—no one ever did—but he had a rough idea where they lay, just beyond the perimeter of the settlement, north of the grazing pastures, east of the field he'd raced in with Egan. The streets were dead as he made his way to the edge of town in the bright moonlight. He felt like a ghost, haunting the pathways and lanes, wandering through a world he no longer felt a part of. Where the last street ended, he could see a line of pathminders spaced distantly from one another, but tracing a clear line before disappearing over a nearby hill. It must be the way, he decided, and followed them through the night.

It didn't take long to reach the hill. Cresting the top, he gasped at the scene on the other side. A wide depression extended below; stretching across its expanse stood what seemed like hundreds of pathminders laid out in a symmetrical grid, bathed in the purple glow of the ringed moon, bright against the plain. He stared in awe at the collection of those who had lived in Harmony, a vast gathering of dead. Normally he would have been frightened at the idea of going down there, but now, standing alone on the hill, he found he wasn't. Delaney was down there and her sounder was with her. He was eager to seek her out and hoped that in reaching her, in singling her out from the unnamed and unremembered dead, he could find some sort of inspiration, some strength to get him through. At the very least, he could say good-bye.

He made his way down the hill, following the path into the valley, and soon reached the edge where the evenly spaced markers began. Taking the finder out of his pocket, he held the device before him, pressed a button, and spoke into it softly.

"Delaney Corrow," he said.

His pulse quickened as a faint tone began to beat its steady rhythm. Starting from his left, he swept the finder across the entire field in a slow arc, waiting for the telltale change in tempo and pitch to point him in the right direction. But something was wrong. As he passed the finder across the middle of the valley, its pitch lowered and the pulsing slowed. Only at the edges did it quicken again, seeming to point him in two directions at once.

*It must be broken*, he thought. Speaking her name a second time, he tried again with the same result. This time, however, he didn't stop at the edge of the cemetery but continued in a circle, and as he rotated to face the other way, the tone, though still faint, grew louder and steadier. Puzzled, he followed its direction as it led him back toward town, switching it to pulse mode, feeling it throb lightly in his hand. As he made his way back into Harmony he realized that the high councilor must have lied. He must still be holding on to her sounder.

Why hadn't he just told Jacob the truth? He would have understood.

But the finder didn't bring him back to her father's house. It steered north and continued west past the center of town, leaving Jacob more and more confused. A half hour later he had reached the storehouses at the edge of Harmony, and still the finder pointed west, drawing him away from the buildings. He stopped a hundred yards out, holding the finder before him, where it continued to throb steadily, leading off into the distance. His heart began to pound so hard he could barely distinguish the finder's throb from his own beating pulse. There was only one explanation. Delaney's father had lied, all right, but not how Jacob had thought. The man had been right in saying he didn't have her sounder, but it wasn't buried in the earth. She had taken it with her. Delaney had run away.

He dropped down into the grass and fell back, his mind spinning with the realization. He could hardly believe it. She had done it, just like she said she would. How did it happen? Had the Seers taken her off? Had she run away like he had upon discovery, only plunging blindly out onto the plains without aid or comfort? Had her father let her go after all? The questions flooded his mind, but in the end they didn't matter. What was important was that she had left, that she was out there somewhere. Best of all, there was the chance that she was still alive.

He sat upright. Maybe *he* should escape, leave now while he still could. Maybe he could find her. If she could do it, why couldn't he? He jumped to his feet and stared out through the moonlight to where the land stretched into nothingness. He hesitated. How could he leave? He had no food, no water, nothing to help him face what was out there. What *was* out there? He had no idea. His entire world was right here, confined to this tiny sphere he'd never traveled more than a few hundred yards beyond, even with his sight. Besides, he wouldn't just be leaving a place. He'd be leaving his family, his community, and his only chance to return to oneness with the collective. Delaney could leave, but she was Delaney. She was strong willed and sure; he wasn't. No matter how well he understood her now, he couldn't make himself be like her. He could only be himself.

Resisting the impulse to hurl the finder far into the grass so that it might be lost forever, he turned his back on the west, full of anguish. She would forgive him. She would understand.

Arriving home, he couldn't bring himself to go back inside. Instead he climbed onto the roof of their dwelling and lay on the damp grass. The great ringed moon was setting, purple against the dark plains. Its smaller sister sat on the other side of the horizon, glowing pink, its craters shadowed. He stared at the zenith and watched the stars drift along. Far above, along the surface of the atmosphere, the dark shadow of a ship punctuated with lights lazily crawled across the sky. Occasionally its jets flared, and the pink moon illuminated its trail of vapor. Jacob watched it for an hour before it disappeared, heading for deeper space. He wondered where it was going.

# CHAPTER FIFTEEN

Jacob lay in bed. He could hear the clattering of plates and silverware filtering through the half-open door and the hushed tones of his parents' conversation. He had closed the door last night after returning to bed; one of them must have opened it this morning. Normally they would have long since awakened him, but today was unlike any other day. This was his last morning as a Seer, his last morning as the boy his parents had just yesterday discovered they had been living with. They now knew him in a way that they would have preferred not to know, just as he knew things about them he'd rather not know. He still loved them. Did they feel the same? It seemed to him that that's what the pain of growing had to offer—you saw things you'd rather not see, you learned things about people that surprised and hurt you, but in the end you still loved them. That's what his sight had taught him. It was a lesson he would soon forget, a lesson Harmony would never know.

Jacob waited, lingering in bed until his father finally came in and asked him to get up. By now an incredible and vaguely familiar aroma had wafted its way to his room. It was the smell of bacon and eggs frying on the stove; the last time he had enjoyed the delicious odor was more than a year ago at Egan's house. He got out of bed, dressed slowly, and went into the kitchen. His mother greeted him warmly, as if he were a guest who had popped in for an overnight visit. Both of his parents seemed cheerful, or tried to, anyway, joking with each other as they used to do when he was younger. He walked through the darkness to the front door and opened it; morning sunlight cascaded in, illuminating the kitchen. His parents, unaware of the change, continued moving about, and as he watched them, Jacob felt invisible, as if he had lifted up a rock to reveal a colony of ants that went about their business, oblivious to a spectator.

"Mind if I leave the door open?" he asked.

"What for?" his mother asked, turning in his direction. "Oh," she realized suddenly, and walked to the stove.

"I like the light," he said. They ignored him; he left it open. The way they pretended to be happy, pretended that nothing was wrong, that nothing important was about to occur, irritated him. Maybe they were happy. After all, they weren't the ones about to undergo surgery, to have their memory erased. As far as they were concerned, they would deliver this strange boy and have their old son returned, brand new.

He stared into the street, watching the morning activities. Cats wandered the lane, sniffing plants. One of them hissed at another over the body of a squeak that still twitched between its paws. People were emerging from their homes, leaving for their work duties. One at a time, as they passed by his yard, they stopped and turned in his direction, tilting their heads to catch a scent of the cooking bacon. He watched their nostrils flare, their throats constrict as they swallowed the saliva that he knew flooded their mouths in response to the aroma. Occasionally two or three gathered and whispered to one another, and he knew their conversation, though he couldn't hear the words. One pair, so distracted by the smells that they failed to hear their sounders chime in proximity, ran into each other. One of them lost balance and tumbled; both cried out in surprise.

"Better watch where you're going," Jacob cried, and laughed as they jumped at his voice, guiltily hurrying away.

"Time to eat, Jake," his mother called from inside. Leaving the door ajar, he went in and sat down. He served them all, spooning the scrambled eggs and bacon onto three chipped plates. He spotted an open can on the table with a spoon sticking out.

"What's in the can?" he asked, though he knew the contents.

"We still have some of the pears," his mother said. "I thought you might like some."

"I'm surprised they didn't take them," he noted.

"I guess I forgot to tell them," she said softly.

"This is quite a breakfast," Jacob said brightly. "Bacon, eggs—"

"The high councilor stopped by this morning and brought them," his father broke in. "I thought it was nice of him. He's a good man."

"One last meal?" Jacob asked. Neither of them answered. He could see their bowed heads in the half-light of the kitchen.

"Would you like some pears?" he asked, taking the can.

"No, thank you," they said in unison.


At noon Jacob's parents accompanied him to the common, where the council and most of the settlement had convened for the Gathering. The three of them were escorted by a pair of listeners who had shown up at his house, the same men who had escorted him from school. Nobody spoke en route to the common. As they approached the main square he could hear the chorus of hundreds of sounders hovering in the air above the crowd. The buzzing tone grew louder as he approached. He hadn't attended a Gathering since gaining his sight, and as he came around the corner into the common, the sight of the multitude gave him pause. They stood sideways to him, facing the stage in the northeast corner of the square. Waves of pale heads, lined up in rows, filled the entire space; hands on backs linked each row, creating a symmetry of human shapes almost identical in their coarse brown garments. Their stillness startled him most, however. He expected a crowd this size to appear as a rippling mass of bobbing heads and reaching arms. These figures, however, could easily be mistaken for statues. All that betrayed them as living beings was the occasional blinking of their eyes and the overwhelming hum of their collective sounders. He could hardly remember being one of them.

A man with a shaved head swung an immense mallet against the hanging gong at the edge of the platform. As its reverberations shivered through the crowd, hands reflexively went to pins and the overtone stopped. The square was silent. Jacob felt his heart pounding in his chest, heard the blood pulsing in his ears.

"Come on, Jacob. The high councilor is waiting for you," one of the listeners said.

They separated him from his parents and led him along the edge of the crowd to the stage. He was ordered onto the platform and climbed the stairs with trembling legs. As he reached the top a single man walked to the middle of the stage and stood facing the crowd. It was the high councilor. Not knowing what else to do, Jacob walked over, then froze as the man turned in his direction. His heart leaped into his throat and he gasped for air. Those pale, inhuman eyes, the long, dark beard streaked with gray. He had seen this face before—it had been burned into his memory three days ago at his doorstep. This was the man his mother had embraced. Seeing his mother with her lover had been terrible enough, but knowing it was *him* was far worse. A bitter tang gathered in Jacob's throat.

The high councilor seemed to sense Jacob's hesitation, oblivious to its cause. "Come here, son. Don't be frightened," the man coaxed.

Jacob slowly walked over, full of regret. *I should've run*, he thought. *I shouldn't be here.* Despite his loathing for Delaney's father for all his betrayals, he felt more contempt for himself at his own weakness. The high councilor placed his hands on Jacob's shoulders; Jacob cringed at the man's touch. The crowd, which had begun shifting and murmuring, aware of Jacob's arrival, settled now into silence as the leader addressed them.

"You are all aware of Jacob's peculiar situation. By now you are also aware of the council's decision. We must all remember that our young friend is not at fault. A mistake occurred, and we will fix it, as we do all mistakes in the community. Jacob will soon be one of us again. We know you will all support Jacob and his family in this ordeal."

Jacob stared at the quiet crowd. They were the people he had grown up with, had learned from, had even admired. Now all he could see were faces that reflected a variety of expressions—sympathy, fear, contempt, blankness. And because he knew most of them only by the sound of their voice, their silence made them strangers to him.

"In a sense, we are fortunate," the high councilor continued, "for this incident provides us an opportunity to realize our good fortune and strengthen our bonds. Jacob's bravery in willingly submitting himself for correction serves as a reaffirmation of our own faith in Truesight. He is an inspiration to us all and reminds us of our duty."

"Blindness is purity. Blindness is unity. Blindness is freedom," the crowd chanted in response.

"The council will now escort Jacob to the ghostbox. You may return to your duties, safe in the knowledge that soon all will once again be normal."

The crowd applauded and music blared from the speakers as Jacob was escorted offstage by the high councilor, who held his hand firmly. They left the square, surrounded by a squad of listeners, with the dozen men and women of the council following behind. The blare of music and clapping hands faded as they paraded through the quiet streets. Everyone remained silent; even their sounders had been deactivated, but for two listeners who marched ahead of them. They headed southeast to the edge of the settlement before following a path away from town toward a dark bunker. Jacob had noticed that building from a distance several times and wondered what it contained, for he had never seen anyone coming from or going to it. Now he knew.

The shaking in his legs renewed as they neared the structure. He took deep breaths to calm himself, not to betray his fright. He wouldn't give them that.

The great doors opened with a loud hydraulic hiss. Martin Corrow ushered Jacob along, and they stepped into a chamber. Everyone else remained outside. Except for the dim glow of computer screens and blinking data banks, the room was unlit. But enough light shone from the open doors that Jacob could survey the scene. The room was mostly empty. To his right he observed two figures silhouetted against the wall, waiting patiently in their long white robes. Between them, a table with straps emerged from the wall; above it hovered several robotic arms like those he had seen on the harvesters in the fields, though these pieces of jointed metal protruding from the wall were much smaller and more delicate.

He gazed toward the center of the room, where the only other object stood before him—a tall, dark obelisk, perfectly rectangular and bare but for a single yellow light shining behind a glass lens. The glowing eye met his gaze, burning into him with cold indifference. He closed his eyes and pictured the first clear image that had greeted him a week ago. In his mind, one black-and-yellow insect bit into the head of its smaller prey.

"Leave us for a moment," the high councilor ordered. As the robed figures left, he turned to Jacob, keeping a firm grip on Jacob's shoulder.

"You've viewed the world through a Seer's eyes. You've seen quite a bit, I'm sure—much more, I suspect, than what you've told us. But it's over, Jacob. Any last words? Any final confessions?" he asked, a hint of humor in his voice that froze Jacob's blood.

"I know," Jacob replied softly but with conviction. As frightened as he was by the room and his purpose there, he no longer felt scared of the man. A glimmer of Delaney's defiance rose up within him as he confronted him with the truth.

"Know what? What are you talking about?" the high councilor demanded.

"I know about Delaney. I know you lied—she's not dead. She ran away."

There was a long pause as the high councilor processed Jacob's words. "You're a clever boy, Jacob. However you found out, it doesn't surprise me. Yes, she ran away, but I doubt she survived."

"You mean she didn't leave with the Seers?" Jacob asked in dismay.

"No. I would never allow that. She wanted independence and I gave it to her. I'm sure she discovered for herself just how far it got her."

"How could you? She was your daughter." He couldn't believe what he was hearing.

The high councilor responded defensively. "She gave me no choice. I tried to change her mind, get her to stay, but she threatened to make our lives intolerable."

"You mean intolerable for *you*."

"For us all. I did what I had to do for the good of the community. She was a blight, an anomaly. Just like you. You, however, are easier to fix."

His words stung Jacob. "You're a liar. Everything about you is a lie. I know."

"You know? You know nothing. You're a boy, and a Seer. Sometimes, Jacob, we have to lie to serve a greater truth. Regardless, you will soon forget all this and Delaney will be dead to you once again, as she is to me and everyone else." Jacob could hear the fury rising in his voice. "I didn't enjoy cutting her out, and it saddens me that it had to be my own daughter, but it was a price I was willing to pay. Now it's time for you to pay yours." He leaned down so that his face was even with Jacob's, and tightened his grip. The eye of the ghostbox cast a yellow pall across his face. "Let's just hope the surgery goes well, Jacob. The ghostbox makes mistakes from time to time."

His lips curled back the slightest bit and his left eye blinked, a slow and knowing wink. Jacob recoiled in shock at the gesture, at what it could only mean. One final, dreadful secret revealed, a secret that enveloped all the others, wrapping them in darkness. *He can see!* he thought in horror.

With a sudden jerk Jacob twisted away from the high councilor's grasp and darted through the doors. After a second of stunned hesitation the high councilor rushed to the doorway, crying for him to stop as the small crowd outside turned in confusion. A squad of listeners, alarmed by the cry, jumped onto the path ahead of Jacob, forming a chain in the hope of catching him. Jacob leaped to one side and, bounding through the tall grass, ran toward the colony.

As he fled he heard the high councilor's voice calling out above the confused clamor: "If you leave, you can never return!"

He kept on running.


He darted through the streets toward home, gasping for air, feeling both terrified and exhilarated from the escape. It had happened so fast, had caught him unaware. The wink had done it, a sly and snide revelation of the man's utter corruption that had broken the spell and set him free. In the end, after everything that had happened, everything he'd learned, it was a single, simple gesture that had enraged him and sent him flying through this long, dark tunnel toward the light. But he had to hurry. It wouldn't take them long to figure out where he had gone and where he might be heading. Reaching his house, he threw open the door and ran inside, searching in the meager light. He opened cupboards and drawers until he spotted the glint of metal cylinders. Three cans of pears remained. He took all three, a block of cheese, and a couple loaves of bread and placed them on the table. Then he grabbed a sharp knife, a cup, a bowl, and an electric lighter and put those on the table as well. Snatching a canvas bag from the closet, he dashed into his room and stuffed his blanket into the satchel along with an extra shirt and towel. He grabbed the finder last, tucked it between the folds of his blanket, and raced back down the hall into the kitchen. He stuffed the food and supplies into the bag, zipped it closed, and slipped the carrying strap over his shoulder. Breathing heavily, he gazed around one last time, took the silver pin from his chest, and placed it on the table. Then he left.

He could hear shouts one street over and the sound of running feet approaching the corner. He quickly crossed the lane and climbed the side of the house opposite his onto the grassy roof, and peered down as a group of five men turned onto the street below him. They immediately headed to his house and burst down the door, disappearing inside. He headed in the opposite direction, running along the ridge of the hill until he reached the end and scrambled down to the street. He hurried through the North Tier, stopping in the small square to drink from the fountain. The square was vacant. Dunking his sweaty head into the pool, he sucked in the cool water with long gulps and then was off again, quickly to the north field, where the faint trails of playful children meandered through the waist-high grass.

He could see the line of pathminders standing tall in the distance, tracing the northern perimeter of the colony. Turning around, he glanced back at the colony that stretched below him. No one was nearby; the streets were empty. Either they were concentrated along the southern gate of the colony or had given up, realizing the futility of the search. He turned back and surveyed the field. Beyond the pathminders the plains stretched to the horizon, row after row of hills disappearing into haze. He would cross that northern line, veer left, and head west, where the transports came from, the large haulers driven by Seers. There were people there, he guessed; how far, he had no idea. Among them, hopefully, was Delaney—if she was still alive, he would find her.

He resisted the urge to turn around, to run home, back into the arms of his mother, back into the cool darkness beneath the earth. Instead he ran down the back side of the hill and into the field, leaping through the grass that separated before him and closed behind, swallowing him up. He broke the line, the pathminders wailed, and the screeching in his ears was almost unbearable. Before long, however, he was far enough away that the noise didn't bother him. Let them wail, he thought. He didn't stop running until he reached the top of the first set of hills nearly a quarter mile away. There he turned around one last time and scanned the edge of the colony that was the only place he had ever known. He thought he saw dark figures standing on the top of the hill. He reached out as if to touch them, then dropped his arm and turned away for good.

# ACKNOWLEDGMENTS

I would first like to thank author Craig Nova—a man writer Garret Keizer once called "the novelist's novelist"—for his considerable advice, wisdom, and warm support throughout the original writing of *Truesight* and beyond. Thanks also to Professor Judy Worman at Dartmouth College for her careful reading and thoughtful line edits during revision, and to Professor Barbara Kreiger for her feedback and support as well.

Thanks are also due to my agent, George Nicholson at Sterling Lord Literistic, for taking an interest in my work and for his skill in finding me a publisher, and to my editor, Susan Rich, at HarperCollins, for her enthusiasm and her great talent in helping me make this a much better book than it might have been otherwise.

I would also like to thank my colleagues at Lyndon Institute for their support throughout this project, in particular English department chair Gerry Stork and headmaster Rick Hilton. Special thanks goes to English teacher John Barksdale for his helpful feedback and suggestions (and even more importantly for his excellent driving skills, which got me to the hospital in time to see the birth of my son).

Finally, I would like to thank my family and friends for their love and encouragement. Most of all, I'd like to thank my wife, Erica, a brilliant freelance editor in her own right, not only for her love and companionship but for her thoughtful ideas and edits throughout the writing of this book